INDIAN PHILOSOPHY A–Z

Forthcoming Volumes in the Philosophy A–Z Series

Indian Philosophy A–Z

Christopher Bartley

Edinburgh University Press

© Christopher Bartley, 2005

Edinburgh University Press Ltd
22 George Square, Edinburgh

Typeset in 10.5/13 Sabon
by TechBooks India, and printed and
bound in Finland by WS Bookwell

A CIP record for this book is
available from the British Library

ISBN 0 7486 2210 1 (hardback)
ISBN 0 7486 2028 1 (paperback)

Contents

Series Editor's Preface

When one examines the vast variety of philosophical views that originated in India, the term 'Indian Philosophy' might seem more accurately replaced by 'Indian philosophies'. This is true of all national terms applied to philosophy, of course, but rarely so true as in the case of Indian philosophy. This got off the ground perhaps as long ago as 1000 BCE with the *Rig Veda*, and developed into highly sophisticated schools of thought linked to a series of religious texts. Then Indian philosophy was boosted by a reaction to *Vedantic* thought by Buddhists and others, and this form of philosophy migrated to the rest of Asia, and beyond. Teachers of the history of philosophy often complain that their students today find it difficult to understand Locke and Hume, even if they are native English speakers. How much more difficult, then, is it for an English-speaking audience to understand the concepts of Indian philosophy, distant as they are from us in time and expressed in an entirely distinct language and culture? Chris Bartley's book is designed to show that the task of explaining Indian philosophical concepts is not as difficult or mysterious as has often been thought. It is the aim of this series to present philosophical terms from different areas of the discipline in accessible and interesting ways, and I welcome this contribution to the task in hand.

Oliver Leaman

Introduction

Students often ask whether they are required to spell Sanskrit words correctly in their written work. The nice response is that they are expected to show that they understand what the (hopefully recognisable) terms mean. This handbook tries to elucidate the focal meanings of concepts that readers of Indian philosophy in English translations are likely to encounter.

It is in the nature of the case that concepts and logical techniques described here are taken out of specific contexts. I have tried to write in such a way that a glance at a particular entry will assist understanding of the way in which a term is being used on a particular occasion.

The existence of this book testifies to a belief that the study of classical Indian philosophical and religious thought is intrinsically worthwhile. These thinkers were concerned with issues of universal significance that are crystallised and discussed with a singular clarity and argumentative precision. It is to be hoped that this book contributes to an acceptance of the view that it makes sense to speak of World Philosophy, of which classical Indian philosophy is a proper part. No one who has read a closely argued Indian philosophical text can deny that the activity was governed by rigorous canons of rationality and a presumption that conclusions must be justified.

The sociologist Louis Dumont maintained that the key to understanding Indian religion is to be found in the dialogue between the person who has renounced society and the participant in everyday social relations. This is surely an important insight. I maintain that the keys to understanding Indian philosophy are to be found in the dialectic between the anti-essentialist Buddhist outlook that reality is to be understood fundamentally as an impersonal process of events from which the notion of individual identities is an abstraction, and the Brahminical Hindu view that it is the interactions between persisting stable identities or substances that generate processes. Further, there is the dialectic between the view that the values encoded in the orthodox hierarchical ideology of social and religious duty (*dharma*) are absolutes and the subversive belief that they are only human constructs. Again, there is the dialectic between the view that the world as represented in the categories of common sense is what it seems (the lotus growing out of the mud) and the conviction that the differences and oppositions that we experience are misconceptions resolvable into a higher unifying synthesis.

About thirty years ago my teacher Julius Lipner expressed the modest aspiration that one of our duties as students of Indian thought was that of helping to dissolve the misconceptions about those traditions current in the West. I hope that this book is a step in the right direction.

Acknowledgements

I would like to thank Loretta Bartley, Stephen Clark, Michael Fry, Jonardon Ganeri, Julius Lipner, Michael McGhee, Oliver Leaman and Mark Siderits for advice and encouragement.

Using This Book

Italic bold signals a cross-reference. The glossary at the end lists some of the current English translations of Sanskrit terms that readers are likely to encounter.

Indian Philosophy A–Z

A

Abhava (absence): considered a basic constituent of reality (*padartha*) by the *Nyaya-Vaisheshikas*, who hold that absences are perceptible. It is always the absence of something known to be real, which is technically termed the *pratiyogin* (counter-positive). That there is no jar on the table translates as, 'there is absence of jar on the table'. This is a true negative fact. If true propositions have actual, objective truth-makers, absences must be realities, although not actualities. The absence of, say, an obstruction, is just as much a reality as the presence of one. Although the hole in the bucket is not a positive entity (*bhava*), being just the absence of some material, it's real enough.

The *Nyaya-Vaisheshika* realists classify absence into four sorts:

> *Prag-abhava* (prior absence) has an end but no beginning. It is the non-existence of any product prior to its origination: for example, the non-existence in curds in milk prior to their formation.
> *Pradhvamsa-abhava* (destruction) has a beginning but no end: the non-existence of milk once the curds have formed.

Atyanta-abhava (unlimited absence): understood as holding in past, present and future, this means impossibilities both logical and physical, for example, the son of a barren woman and the hare's horn.

Anyonya-abhava (mutual absence) is difference: the denial of identity between two things such as the pot and the cloth and the assertions that fire differs from water and the table is not the pot. This need not involve perception.

See *anupalabdhi-pramana*

Further reading: G. Bhattacharya 1989; Ingalls 1951; Kajiyama 1998; Matilal 1968

Abhidharma: a style of literary composition and analytical method, practised by some early Buddhist schools, *Abhidharma* is the systematisation of Buddhist ideas that were presented discursively in the Buddha's sermons, in the Pali Canon. These texts, compiled between 100 BCE and 400 CE by various Buddhist schools, are exhaustive catalogues of the mental and material atoms (*dharma*) that are the building blocks of all persons, experiences and objects. Although each *dharma* is said to be independent of all others and self-sufficient, the increasingly complex *Abhidharma* catalogues classify them so that they appear interdependent.

It is a fundamental Buddhist principle that nothing compounded, conditioned, or consisting of parts is ultimately real. The human mind conventionally interprets a combination of parts as a single entity with an enduring nature because this outlook suits our needs. The *Abhidharmikas* held that the atoms are ultimately real entities (*paramartha-sat*/*dravya-sat*). They thought that the *dharmas*' possession of intrinsic natures or essences (*svabhava*) distinguished them from the compound entities that they make up. Essence here means a nature that is timeless, unchanging, permanent, self-sufficient and independent of anything else. Such an identity would be uncaused. Acceptance of essence implies the existence of types of entities. Each atomic factor has two modes of existence: actualised and non-actualised. Each exists with its nature or essence unchanging (*svabhava*) and independently of everything else in a timeless dimension, but the atoms are momentarily actualised as and in the cosmos, including the temporary streams of experiences that we all call persons. The patterns formed by the atoms lend themselves to our conceptually constructing a worldview involving individual, personal subjects of experience and the stable environment that they inhabit.

The *Abhidharma* writings differentiate those atomic factors that are spiritually unhelpful from those that are virtuous. Through insight one can remove defilements and approach enlightenment. The skilled meditator analyses his experiences into their fleeting components, thus dissolving the objects of attachment and eliminating desires for them. Through the same process he realises that there is no soul or permanent identity, just currents in an ocean of experiences.

See *Vaibhashika*

Further reading: Frauwallner 1995; Potter 1996; Pruden 1988

Abhihita-anvaya-vada: the view of *Kumarila* and his followers that each individual word has its own innate meaning. When these meanings are combined in accordance with the rules of grammar, they produce the purport (*tatparya*) of the sentence. In isolation, words primarily express features shared by a group of entities: they refer to something specific when interrelated in sentences.

Further reading: Brough 1996b; Matilal 1990; Mohanty 1992

Abhinavagupta (975–1025 CE): a Kashmiri theologian and aesthetician, *Abhinavagupta* belonged to the **Tantric Trika** ritual cult, whose doctrines, *yoga* and rituals he expounded in his *Tantraloka*. His major philosophical works are commentaries on **Utpaladeva**'s *Ishvarapratyabhijna-karikas* and the *Malinivijayottara Tantra*. These works present critiques of the dualism of the **Shaiva Siddhanta** ritualism, *Vedantic* illusionism that maintains that all normal human experience is infected by ignorance of the truth about reality and the Buddhist rejection of persisting essences, including the soul. Basic to his outlook is a belief that other doctrinal systems are not to be treated as opponents but as aspects of the self-expression of the supreme conscious reality. He formulates a single hierarchy of belief systems in accordance with how closely they approximate to the view that ultimate reality is dynamic universal consciousness.

Abhinavagupta propounded a form of absolute idealism according to which the world derives from a single universal, autonomous (*svatantrya*) and dynamic consciousness that expresses itself in an infinite variety of subjects, objects and acts of awareness. Only ideas are real. The seeker after release from rebirth is to meditate upon the nature of consciousness, oscillating between the illumination of objects (*prakasha*) and reflective awareness (*vimarsha*). In ordinary individual awareness, the representation of what are taken to be external objects, and hence duality, predominates. The adept should reflect that experience of objectivity is just experience or consciousness expressing itself. The subject–object polarity is understood as internal to consciousness. When one realises that the polarity is but a construction within the one consciousness, contracted self-awareness is dissolved along with thinking about the world in terms of external objects, individual subjectivity and agency, and god.

Following *Somananda* and *Utpaladeva*, *Abhinav-agupta* believes that the mind-independence of matter is impossible. Trans-individual consciousness causes the manifestations that we experience to appear as if distinct from the subjects of experience. While *Advaita-Vedanta* understands the foundational consciousness in static terms, for this school it is self-conscious activity and will positing itself as apparently other than itself. It operates through projecting manifestations (*abhasa*) that are the contents of our experiences.

Against Buddhism he argues for the self-conscious subject (*atman*), the permanent background to experience, persisting as a stable unity that synthesises mental states. Without such a principle, there would only be momentary, self-contained, unrelated mental episodes. The key to understanding his philosophy is to be found in his critique of the notion that our ideas represent physical objects. He argues that consciousness can only represent what is itself conscious. We only know our experiences. It makes no sense to say that consciousness represents what is mind-independent because as soon as something is represented by consciousness it is no longer mind-independent.

Bondage to rebirth (*samsara*) is a state of ignorant self-limitation that understands the orthodox values of purity and impurity as objective. Liberation from rebirth consists in the recognition, typically through *yoga* and meditation, of oneself as a contracted form of the universal consciousness. Liberation is just this awareness: it is not a separate phenomenon produced by knowledge.

Further reading: Ingalls, Masson and Patwardhan 1990; Kahrs 1998; Padoux 1990; Pandey 1986; Sanderson 1992

Abhranta (unerring, reliable): Buddhists following *Dharmakirti* say that immediate perceptual sensation, which relates to the flux of particular instantaneous realities (*svalakshana*), is free from conceptualisation and is reliable. In fact, assuming that the senses are operating normally, it cannot be either true or false because truth and falsity apply only to conceptual mental states (*vikalpa*). Perceptual sensation applies to reality as it is in itself (*vastu*) before we start to thinking about it. The particular realities are not the direct object of thought and language. Once we start thinking, we can decide whether or not something falls under a given concept. When the senses are confronted by some actuality, the question of whether it exists or not simply does not arise. There is no scope for affirmation and negation. From sensory impressions arise mental images (*akara*) about which the mind forms concepts. If the mental image does not conform to reality, the conceptual thought will be false. Its falsity will be revealed in unsuccessful practice.

Further reading: Stcherbatsky 1993

Abhuta-parikalpa (imaginative construction of the unreal): Buddhists belonging to the idealist *Vijnanavada* school hold that everything is mental and that what we take to be external physical realities are creations of consciousness. There are no external realities that are grasped by thoughts. In reality, there are no enduring subjects of thoughts either. The dichotomy between thinking subjects and external objects is a construction by the thinking mind. It has a purely imaginary nature (*parikalpita-svabhava*). Belief in external objects and enduring thinkers is called the imagination of the unreal (*abhuta-parikalpa*). To the unenlightened mentality, ideas appear to stand for external things. *Abhuta-parikalpa* is also called the dependent nature of things (*paratantra-svabhava*) as conceived by unenlightened people. The unchanging light of consciousness (*prakasha-matra*),

unsullied by mental images, is what is real. This supra-
normal awareness (*lokottara-jnana*) is enlightenment and
it is called the real nature (*parinishpanna-svabhava*).

Further reading: Stcherbatsky 1970; Williams 1989;
Wood 1991

Adarshana-matra: according to the Buddhist ***Dharmakirti***'s
theory of inference, the invariable association (***vyapti***) between the logical reason or proving property (***hetu***) and
the property to be proved (***sadhya***) must be based on a
form of natural regularity (***svabhava-pratibandha***). This
connection may be that of an established causal relation
(fire and smoke) or identity of essence (***tadatmya***) as when
we reason that if something is an oak (***hetu***), then it is a
tree (***sadhya***).

Dharmakirti's teacher ***Ishvarasena*** thought that our
constant association of the logical reason and the ***sadhya*** was based merely on the fact of our not having observed any exceptions to the rule (***adarshanamatra***). For
Dharmakirti, this makes the basis of inference too fragile:
why should we not discover an exception in the future?
Moreover, we have not surveyed every relevant instance.
We do not know that there is no instance where the ***hetu***
occurs and the ***sadhya*** does not. We just have not come
across one so far. So he argued that the inseparability
of ***hetu*** and ***sadhya*** had to be grounded in some natural regularity (***svabhava-pratibandha***). This means that
the presence of the logical reason guarantees the presence
of the property to be proved. There can be no counter-
example.

Further reading: Kajiyama 1998; Tillemans 1999

Adhyasa (superimposition): the ***Advaita Vedantin Shankara***
takes it for granted that what is subjective (that is, consciousness) and what is objective are essentially opposed

and cannot really be related. So it is a mistake to superimpose whatever is objective on the subject and vice versa. But we naturally fail to discriminate the subjective and the objective in so far as we misunderstand ourselves as embodied individual agents participating in normal social and economic life. Two-way superimposition is the failure to distinguish the true inner self from one's embodied life, mind, will and social status. This false identity as agent and experiencer is existential ignorance. The mutual superimposition of the subjective and the objective, called ignorance, is the condition of behaviour involving objects and means of knowledge, secular and religious acts and all the scriptures, whether concerned with ritual actions or with final release.

Further reading: Halbfass 1995; Potter 1981

Adhyavasaya (judgement): Buddhists in the tradition of *Dignaga* and *Dharmakirti* think that objective reality (*vastu, paramartha-sat*) consists of unique, indescribable momentary particulars (*svalakshana*). It is the object of sensory impressions. It is also incommunicable as such. But the mind gives meaning to the impressions received from the realities, which it organises in concepts. *Adhyavasaya* involves the structuring of the information supplied by the senses in such way that it can be converted into action and be communicated. It is what enables us to reach or obtain the real world. Once concepts have been formed they may also be used in inferences. *Dharmakirti* is acutely aware that we frequently forget that our concepts are just convenient representations and treat them as copies of reality as it is in itself. The *Nyaya* and *Samkhya* schools use the term to means the specific determination of the object of thought. For the former it is a property of the principle of identity (*atman*). For the latter it is a function of the mind–matter composite or *buddhi*, that is merely observed by the conscious principle (*purusha*).

Further reading: Mookerjee 1975; Tillemans 1999

Advaita-Vedanta (theory that reality is non-differentiated): this is the religious philosophy of one who has renounced (*samnyasa*) involvement in everyday life and public religion in order to devote himself to salvation. It is a tradition of scriptural interpretation holding that the *Upanishads* teach that the self-revealing (*svasamvedana*) and self-established (*svatah siddha*) soul (*atman*), which is the constant witness (*sakshin*) of all mental events, is identical with the Authentic Reality or *Brahman*, understood as unconditioned (*nirvishesha*) being and tranquil consciousness. Self-illuminating consciousness, the only undeniable reality, is foundational. Inactive pure consciousness has neither objects nor content: it is beyond all oppositions, such as that between knower and known.

This outlook reflects the solitary meditator's introverted experience of undifferentiated awareness. It expresses a conviction that behind the world of variability and becoming is a state of changeless pure being that has nothing in common with the processes that we experience.

The appearance of a manifold cosmos consisting of differences between subjects, agents and objects of experience is blamed on a power of illusion or misconception (*avidya*) that generates the misapprehension of the self as a personal agent subject to Vedic social and ritual duties and transmigration (*samsara*). This ignorance is removed by intuitive insight into the identity of the soul and the featureless Absolute beyond oppositions, preceded by the renunciation of agency that presupposes belief in the reality of differences.

The most important early theorists are *Gaudapada* (450–500 CE), *Mandana Mishra* (650–700 CE) and *Shankara* (c. 700 CE). *Sureshvara* probably belongs to the generation after *Shankara* and his major works are the *Naishkarmyasiddhi* and an exposition of *Shankara*'s commentary on the *Brihadaranyaka Upanishad*.

Other important thinkers are *Padmapada*, *Prakashatman*, and *Vimuktatman*.

See *Adhyasa*; *Bhava-rupa-avidya*; *Neti Neti*

Further reading: Gerow 1990; Halbfass 1995; Hiriyanna 1993; Potter 1981; Ram-Prasad 2002

Ahamkara (egoism and will): according to the *Samkhya* description of the world, which is accepted by *Vedanta*, this is one of the constituents of human personality closely associated with the sense faculties and intellect. It usually means the sort of selfishness that results from identifying the soul (*atman*) with one's embodied life.

Further reading: Rocher 1988

Ahimsa (lack of desire to harm): this is a central idea in Indian religious culture. The *Laws of Manu*, which describes the social and religious duties obligations (*dharma*) to be performed by higher-caste Hindus concerned with preserving spiritual purity in a world permeated by polluting forces, states that *ahimsa* is a duty for Brahmins. The *Yoga-Sutra* (2.30) stipulates that *ahimsa* is one of the five forms of self-restraint (*yama*) to be exercised by practitioners of *Yoga*. Avoiding taking life is one of the five basic precepts undertaken by all Buddhists. Non-violence was promoted as an ideal by the Emperor *Ashoka* (272–232 BCE), a convert to Buddhism, who conquered and ruled much of the Indian sub-continent. It is a fundamental ethical principle in *Jainism,* which takes non-violence to the extremes, regarding even the unintentional killing of an insect as a defect.

Although the principle of non-violence is sometimes upheld as a moral universal, this actually runs counter to traditional orthodoxy that understands the *Vedic dharma*-prescriptions as different for each caste and station of life (*ashrama*). They are not reducible to a single basic principle. In fact, the *dharma*-rules approve certain acts of killing, specifically in the context of sacrificial rituals. Moreover, fighting and killing are included in the caste-duties of *Kshatriya* warriors.

Considerations of pleasure and pain are irrelevant to the determination of what is right and wrong: the only source of knowledge about *dharma*-values are the injunctions and prohibitions found in the eternal and infallible Vedic revelation. Non-Vedic considerations such as pleasure and pain or the promptings of individual conscience are irrelevant. While orthodoxy forbids certain acts of killing and injuring, such prohibitions cannot be universalised since they are relative to a context of action. From, 'It is wrong to kill Brahmins' one cannot infer the general proposition, 'It is wrong to kill'. Killing that is prescribed as a part of a ritual and which is performed in a spirit of 'duty for duty's sake' will not have negative consequences for the agent. In short, the *Veda* as the supreme source of values, cannot itself be evaluated by extra-Vedic considerations.

Further reading: Halbfass 1991; O'Flaherty 1991

Akasha (atmosphere, ether): according to *Vaisheshika,* a type of basic substance (*dravya*). It is the vehicle of sounds, unitary, present wherever there are physical objects, eternal in that it lacks beginning and end, and imperceptible.

Akriti: the physical structure common to a natural kind (*jati*) of entities. It manifests the generic property shared by them. *Samsthana* has the same meaning.

Alambana (objective ground): according to direct realists, the objective ground of a thought is whatever in the world it is about. An objective ground is both the extra-mental cause and the representative content of an idea. A hallucination is not an objectively grounded thought: it has content but it is caused by some defect in the perceptual system. Similarly, a rainbow is not caused by bands of colour but by light reflected in drops of moisture.

In his *Alambana-pariksha*, the Buddhist **Dignaga** tries to refute the atomic theory of the **Abhidharma** Buddhists by calling into question this notion of objective grounding. They think that we directly perceive structured masses of real atoms of various kinds. **Dignaga** questions the possibility of atomic aggregation. But even granting that collections of atoms may cause mental representations, they do not figure in the subjective content of awareness. A compound of clay atoms may cause the perception of a pot, but we do not see a cluster of atoms. What we have is an experience of a solid, coloured, extended object. **Dignaga** concludes that only an idea (a mental image that appears as if external) can be the support of another idea. It may be both instrumental in bringing about the idea and match its representational content.

Further reading: Ganeri 2001a; Matilal 1986

Alata-cakra (whirling firebrand): symbol used by Buddhists to illustrate the way in which consecutive similar elements of existence, although existing only for a moment, succeed each other with such inconceivable rapidity that illusions of substantial continuity are generated. This raises the question that if unity is wrongly superimposed on successive similar moments, what is making the mistake if there is no permanent knowing subject?

Alaya-vijnana: early Buddhism rejects belief in the soul (*atman*) and analyses human lives into five constituents: matter, sensations, perceptions, habits and thoughts. Nevertheless, they accept the *karma* theory that motivated and intentional actions generate good and bad latent potencies that must be exhausted in future spheres of experience. In the absence of a soul, there has to be some other factor that serves as the vehicle of those potentialities. The *Vijnanavada* school postulated a 'storehouse consciousness' (*alaya-vijnana*) as the receptacle for these latent energies produced by morally significant actions. In addition, the contents of awareness, perceptions of an external world, memories and dreams are held to derive from a beginningless supply of residual traces of experience (*vasana*) in the form of latent mental states and dispositions of character preserved in this underlying subconscious level of mind. It also generates the illusion of a real, stable, individual subject confronting a world of objects. The *alaya-vijnana* consisting of a series of thoughts and *karmic* 'seeds' accounts for the continuity of individual personality through death and the transition between lives and in spells of unconsciousness.

A stream of experiences (which we misinterpret as a person's life) consists of a vast store of latent mental impressions (*vasana*) left by previous ideas that inevitably come to fruition. In the beginningless series of births, ideas and their impressions are mutually related as causes and effects, as plants spring from seeds and seeds from plants. The variety of ideas arises from the variety of impressions just as the variety of ideas in dreams arises from mental impressions in the absence of external objects.

Anaikantika-hetu (inconclusive reason): one of the major types of logical fallacy (*hetvabhasa*). There are three varieties:

1. When the logical reason (*hetu*) occurs in cases where what is to be proved (*sadhya*) is absent (that is, it occurs in *vipakshas*).
   Example: the village is holy, because it is close to the Ganges. But there are unholy things close to the Ganges. This is called *Sadharana-hetu*.
2. Where the logical reason only applies to the subject (*paksha*) of the inference (*Asadharana-hetu*). Example: sounds (*paksha*) are impermanent (*sadhya*), because they are audible (*hetu*). It is a condition of an inference's validity that we should be able to cite an instance (*sapaksha*) other than the subject of the inference where both the logical reason and the property to be proved always occur together. But this is impossible here because nothing other than sounds have the property of audibility.
3. Where the subject of the inference is universal. For example 'Everything is nameable, because it is knowable'. The invariable association is, 'Whatever is knowable is nameable'. Distinct from the universal subject, there can be neither a *sapaksha* nor a *vipaksha*, showing the invariable association (*vyapti*) between the logical reason and what is to be proved. Since the inference begins from a question about whether nameability applies to the subject, the invariant association 'whatever is knowable is nameable' is itself doubtful.

Further reading: G. Bhattacharya 1989; Potter and Bhattacharya 1993

Anatta (no soul): Buddhists deny that the subject of thoughts, feelings, actions and their consequences is a permanent, changeless, unified and eternal substance or Soul (*atman*). Thoughts, sensations, emotions and actions undoubtedly occur but this should not be interpreted as implying the existence of a constant subject as a further fact over and above the stream of experiences. Belief in one's own identity is a form of selfish clinging that leads to suffering and anxiety. Early Buddhism reduces individual personality to a stream of five causally interdependent and ever-changing psycho-physical components (*skandhas*); matter, feelings, perceptions, dispositions and thoughts which neither collectively nor singly amount to an enduring substantial self or soul.

As the tradition developed, the cosmos was understood as a basically impersonal process of events rather than as the interaction of persisting entities. It is a misconception, arising from human convenience, that there really are any enduring entities, including selves. Whatever is conventionally considered as a stable continuant is reductively analysed as a stream of occurrences, a flux of impersonal physical and mental atomic factors. This implies that there is no real distinction between enduring substrates and their properties. What makes for the continuity of a person's life is just the occurrence of a series of suitably interconnected physical and mental factors. Such a series constructs an awareness of itself as a persisting centre of experience and agency. This fabrication becomes selfish, alienated from others and protective of its own interests that it anxiously promotes.

Further reading: Collins 1982; Gethin 1998; Rahula 1969; Siderits 2003

Anavastha (infinite regress): this is not technically a logical fallacy, but it indicates that a particular argument can never be proved. Cases include the claim that a cognitive state needs to be the object of another cognitive state before the subject knows that he is in it; that the truth of a thought needs to be confirmed by another thought; and that if two items are joined by a real relation (a third factor), further relations are required to relate the primary relation to the two items and so forth.

Anekanta-vada: while *Nyaya-Vaisheshika* develops a complex scheme of categories (*padartha*) in terms of which we may make sense of objects in the cosmos, *Jainism* claims that we can understand entities using just two factors of analysis: permanence (*dravya*) and change (*paryaya*). *Dravya* means what is unitary and constant. *Paryayas* are particular states that may be present or absent in substances. Reality is too complex to be pinned down in categorical schemes involving strict boundaries. Objects are constants *and* variables. Moreover, given that we are not omniscient, we are not in a position to frame an absolutely correct conception about anything. All our understanding is partial and from a limited perspective. The Jains attempt to convey the ambiguity or indeterminacy of reality relative to human viewpoints in the following logical scheme (where 'it' stands for anything and the square brackets for any feature):

1. In a sense, it is [...]
2. In a sense, it is not [...]
3. In a sense, it both is [...] and is not [...]
4. In a sense, it is inexpressible
5. In a sense, it is [...] and is inexpressible
6. In a sense, it is not [...] and it is inexpressible
7. In a sense, it is [...] and is not [...], and it is inexpressible.

Take the question of whether the soul is embodied. The following are rationally defensible points of view. In a sense, it is. In a sense, it is not (because it can exist without the body). In a sense, it both is and is not embodied. We might not want to claim that it is simultaneously embodied and disembodied (4). We might allow that it is embodied, and not want to claim that it is simultaneously embodied and disembodied (5). We might allow that it is disembodied, and not want to claim that it is simultaneously embodied and disembodied (6). We might allow that there is a sense in which it is both embodied and disembodied and not want to claim that it is simultaneously embodied and disembodied (7).

This technique is applied in debates with Buddhists and Hindu schools of thought. It aims to show that their dogmatic outlooks are at best partial.

Further reading: Ganeri 2001a; Matilal 1981; Radhakrishnan and Moore 1957

Anirvacaniya-khyati (inexplicability of cognitive error): *Advaita Vedantins* think that the content of a cognitive error, such as mistaking a rope for a snake or a piece of shell for silver, cannot be readily characterised as either real or unreal. The rope is real. The mental representation of the snake, in which a memory of a snake is superimposed upon the rope, occurs convincingly and has effects. But the representation turns out to be false. The representation of the snake is not real because it is corrected by the true representation of the rope. The fact that it had actual consequences means that it cannot be treated as non-existent. So the delusory experience is held to be indescribable or indeterminable as real or unreal. This theory is applied on the macrocosmic level. *Advaitins* after *Shankara* think that there is a supernatural force called causal ignorance (*karana-avidya*) that projects all subjects and objects of experience and conceals the true nature of the Absolute Reality (*Brahman*) with which one's soul (*atman*) is ultimately identical. Just as the snake was

mistakenly superimposed upon the real rope, so everything that we experience is superimposed upon Brahman,
which is concealed by the world of every day life. All ordinary experience (*vyavaharika*) is ultimately indescribable as real or unreal. It is not an illusion or hallucination (*pratibhasika*), although not the genuine article
(*paramartha-sat*).

The truth is realised in intuitive insight, rather than by
discursive and conceptual understanding, into the identity of **Brahman**, the undifferentiated reality that is unchanging tranquil consciousness, and the soul that is one's
essential being.

Further reading: Halbfass 1995; Matilal 1986; Ram-
Prasad 2002; Thrasher 1993

Antarvyapti (intrinsic entailment): in a valid inference, the invariable association (*vyapti*) between the logical reason
(*hetu*) and what is to be proved (*sadhya*) is pivotal.

Following **Dignaga**, most Buddhist logicians specified
three features of a valid inference:

1. The reason must be present in the subject (*paksha*).
2. The reason must be present with the *sadhya* in an instance distinct from but relevantly similar to the subject
   (*sapaksha*).
3. There is no instance where the logical reason is present
   and the property to be proved is absent (*vipaksha*).

Where there are positive instances of the invariable association, and instances where both the property to be proved
and the reason are absent, there is what is called external pervasion (*bahirvyapti*). But this is problematic when
the subject of the inference is universal: for example, 'all
realities are momentary because existence means being

causally active'. Here there can be no genuine *sapaksha*, which is distinct from the all-encompassing subject. So it appears that there can be no inferential knowledge of the momentariness of reality. The response of Buddhists such as *Ratnakarashanti* and *Ratnakirti* is that there are cases where the invariant association of the logical reason and *sadhya* is known only in the subject and there is no need of examples by the intelligent. This is called *antarvyapti*. But most Buddhist logicians insist on the need for examples (*bahirvyapti*).

The idea derives from *Jaina* logicians who held that for the relation between reason and property to be proved, it must be a natural one reflecting the nature of things. Whenever an invariable association is recognised, it can be understood in relation to the *hetu* and *sadhya* alone without reference to any other concrete instances.

See *Trairupya-hetu*

Further reading: Kajiyama 1998; Mookerjee 1975; Tillemans 1999

Anubhava (present experience): the *Nyaya-Vaisheshikas* say that thoughts (*buddhi*) may be present experiences and memories (*smriti*). If a present experience has been brought about by one of the instruments of valid cognition (*pramana*), it is a case of knowledge (*prama*). Otherwise it is a case of doubt, error or suppositional reasoning (*tarka*). Memories are not instances of knowledge although they may or may not correspond to the object recollected. This is because one of the conditions that a thought has to satisfy to qualify as knowledge is that it has to yield new information.

The term often refers to the immediate awareness of oneself as a persisting subject of experience.

Further reading: G. Bhattacharya 1989

Anumana (inference): a reliable instrument of knowledge (*pramana*) about something that is beyond the senses. It requires cognitions (*jnana*) arising from sensory perceptions. According to the *Nyaya* realism, it begins with a doubt, such as whether there is a fire on a remote mountain. The relevant observation is that we can see smoke. In this case, fire is technically called the *sadhya* – that which is to be established or the property to be proved. The mountain is called the subject (*paksha*) and the smoke is called the logical reason (*hetu*) in the inferential process. We already know that there is no smoke without fire (this invariable association is called *vyapti*) from familiar instances such as the kitchen. By way of corroboration, we also know the truth of the contraposed version of the generalisation: 'no fire, no smoke' from cases like the lake. We apply knowledge of the general principle to the case in question and can safely conclude that there is indeed fire on the mountain although we do not see the fire.

A demonstrative inference (*prayoga*) used to persuade someone else (*parartha-anumana*) would be formulated by the *Nyaya-Vaisheshikas* as:

Statement of the position or uncertainty (*pratijna*): 'There is fire (*sadhya*) on the mountain (*paksha*).'

Logical reason (*hetu*): Because there is smoke on the mountain.

General principle (*vyapti*): 'Wherever there is smoke, there is fire' that is supported by evidence – like a kitchen (*sapaksha*); unlike a lake (*vipaksha*).'

Application (*upanaya*): 'There is smoke on the mountain', which states that the subject has the logical reason that is always associated with (pervaded by or included in – *vyapta*) the property to be proved.

Conclusion (*nigamana*): Therefore, there is fire.

If the statement of *vyapti* is a universal law, the inference is deductively valid. Logical fallacies are termed 'bogus reasons' (*hetvabhasa*).

See *svabhava-pratibandha*

Further reading: G. Bhattacharya 1989; Ganeri 2001b; Matilal 1998

Anupalabdhi-hetu (negative inference): the Buddhist *Dharmakirti* extensively elaborated varieties of this valid form of inference. Examples:

> 'There is no smoke here, because it is not perceived. Smoke being in principle perceptible (*upalabdhi-lakshana-prapta*), it would be perceived were it present.'
> 'There is no soul, because it is not cognised' (*Svabhava-anupalabdhi*).
> 'The causes of smoke do not occur here, because there is no smoke' (*karya-anupalabdhi*).
> 'There is no smoke here, because there is no fire' (*karana-anupalabdhi*).
> 'There are no oaks here, because there are no trees' (*vyapaka-anupalabdhi*).
> 'There is no feeling of cold here, because there is fire' (*svabhava-viruddha-upalabdhi*).

See *drishya-anupalabdhi*

Further reading: Kajiyama 1998; Prasad 2002

Anupalabdhi-pramana (non-cognition as a reliable means of knowledge): not cognising something, that is, cognising an absence (*abhava*), is recognised by the *Purva Mimamsaka Kumarila* and some *Advaita-Vedantins* as a means of acquiring knowledge (*pramana*). It is different from perception and inference.

The puzzling question 'How do we know something if it isn't there?' can be rephrased as, 'How can we know that something is absent?' Realists say that a true cognition must have real object (*prameya*). But the absence of something does not seem to be an object. Conversely, if it is an object, can it really be an absence? *Kumarila* held that an absence is a real entity (*vastu*) in that it is a real aspect of the perceptual situation. He says that an entity can be known as what it is and as what it is not, in accordance with its own features and the things from which it differs. So not being a cloth is a real aspect of a pot. This sort of non-being is a reality that is known not by perception but by another reliable means of knowledge called non-cognition (*anupalabdhi*). He says that this concept of absence and non-cognition help us to understand the real differences between objects.

Perception apprehends the positive aspects of a situation – what is there – but what is missing (for example, the pot's handle) is rightly apprehended by non-cognition (which must involve memory of something real that is the absentee or *pratiyogin*)

The *Prabhakara-Mimamsakas* do not think that absences are realities and so don't need a *pramana* for them. Cognition of absence is just having a mental image of something potentially perceptible that is not presented to the senses.

Further reading: Hiriyanna 1993; Suryanarayana Sastri 1942

Anuvyavasaya: the *Nyaya* school holds that many psychological episodes pass unnoticed. That is to say, information may be received from the environment via the senses, processed by the mind (*manas*) and stored in the memory without being consciously registered. The elevation to explicit conscious awareness of an item of informational input is termed *anuvyavasaya*. This happens when one cognitive state become the object of another. An objection is that if the elevation to consciousness of an informational state requires another psychological state, an infinite regress (*anavastha*) results.

Further reading: Matilal 1986

Anvaya-vyatireka: a mode of reasoning (*yukti*) stating that when A is present, B is present, and when A is absent, B is absent. This is used to establish a relation of cause and effect. For example: given that we see that our own actions happen after our intentions and that they do not happen in the absence of our intentions, there is a causal connection between intention and the occurrence of action. The causal relation is established by perception and nonperception and consists in positive and negative agreement.

Anvaya-vyatireka-vyapti (positive and negative positive pervasion) is rather different and involves logical contraposition. That is to say: if A is *pervaded* by (or included in the scope of) B, whenever A occurs, B occurs and whenever B is absent, A is absent. Taking A as smoke and B as fire we have the positive state of affairs (*anvaya*): 'Where there is smoke, there is fire (as in a kitchen)' and the negative one (*vyatireka*): 'Where there is no fire there is no smoke (as in a lake).'

See *Hetu*

Further reading: G. Bhattacharya 1989; Halbfass 1991

Anvita-abhidhana (related designation): the ritual theorist *Prabhakara* thinks that word meanings are primarily understood when related to actions and events rather than when referring to already existent objects. So the fabric of linguistic understanding consists of sentences that include a verb-meaning, not of isolated words. All meanings are relative to particular situations. A child does not learn individual words on their own but learns language through the insertion and removal of words in sentences. She hears, 'bring a cow' and sees someone do that. Then she hears, 'bring a horse'. By the removal and insertion of words in sentences, she learns the meanings of individual words.

'Related designation' may also be interpreted as the view that it is only in the context of a sentence that a word has meaning: when we want to know the meaning of a word, we should look at its use in context and not scrutinise it in isolation.

Further reading: Brough 1996b; Matilal 1990; Mohanty 1992

Anyatha-khyati (cognition of something as other than it is): the explanation of mistaken cognition according to *Nyaya-Vaisheshika* and *Kumarila*. Assuming that the sensory receptors are operating efficiently, immediate perceptual sensation cannot be false. It pertains solely to the objective realm and involves no subjective interpretation. These realists deny that the objective world is reflected in consciousness that may act as a distorting mirror or that the mind is programmed with ideas that condition what we perceive. They reject the view that the contents of cognitive errors are subjective inventions.

When a piece of shell is mistaken for silver, there is perception of a shiny surface. This may elicit a memory of silver. This true memory of real silver is confused with the current awareness of what is presented to the senses due to the similarity of the surface appearances of shell and silver. That is to say, we do not notice the difference between two representations: one relating to the present object and the other relating to previously seen silver. The error does not arise because we superimpose purely subjective imaginations on what is given. The representation of silver refers to real silver.

Explanation of cognitive error without admitting that ideas may lack reference to real objects is also a feature of *Prabhakara*'s theory of error.

Further reading: Hiriyanna 1993; Matilal 1986

Apoha-vada ('exclusion of the other': Buddhist theory of meaning): realists think that objective general features (universal properties, natural kinds, quality-types such as blues, red, shapes and sizes, and action types) serve as the basis for the repeated applications of general terms or predicates. On this view we classify some individual animals as cows because they form a natural kind. The property 'being a cow' is itself an entity common to all cows. But Buddhists, such as *Dignaga* and *Dharmakirti*, deny that there are any objective generalities structuring and causally regulating reality that consists of instantaneous unique and indescribable particulars (*svalakshana*). If there are neither shared properties nor even resemblances, how do words and concepts operate?

The answer is that word-meanings and concepts 'exclude the other'. While there is no positive property shared by all individual cows, what all cows have in common is their being different from whatever is not a cow. We apply a meaning such as 'cow' just on the basis of the difference of cows from everything else. This 'difference from non-cows' is not a positive feature or a resemblance. It is at best a boundary. The word 'cow' does not stand for a property or essence. We sort some particulars when it suits human interests. Language is a network of mutually exclusive meanings that we have conventionally constructed in accordance with what matters for us. To illustrate: we apply the word 'analgesic' to a variety of pills with totally distinct pharmacological properties because they relieve pain. The concept 'analgesic' is a humanly constructed one because pain relief is a matter of interest to us.

See *Adhyavasaya, Kalpana*

Further reading: Kajiyama 1998; Matilal 1986; Siderits 1991 and 2003; Stcherbatsky 1993; Tillemans 1999

Artha: like the English word 'meaning', this is an ambiguous term. Either it may be an object in the world that is the referent of a linguistic expression (the thing meant) or it may be the meaning (the sense) of a word, sentence or context. It also stands for the overall import of a body of literature such as a group of scriptures or some systematic teaching (*shastra*). It may mean purpose or goal. It may also mean property, wealth and possessions (one's *things*). Failure to attend to the word's equivocal nature sometimes leads to mistakes in translation. Sometimes *vishaya* is used for mental content or representation (or the object-as-cognised) and *artha* for the object external to the mind. But there is no hard and fast rule here.

There are different views about what is the *artha* (meaning and thing meant) of a word. The grammarians say that in normal language a noun refers to an individual object (*dravya, vyakti*) by convention. The *Purva-Mimamsaka* tradition, which explains the texts dealing with rituals, holds that a noun primarily refers to a class or entities (*jati*) or to the shape or form (*akriti*) that they have in common. The relation between word and meaning is innate and eternal. Words have to be used in sentences if they are to refer to individuals. The *Nyaya-Vaisheshikas* say that a word refers to an individual qualified by a class property. Reference and the word meaning relation is a human convention

See *Lakshana-artha*

Further reading: Ganeri 1999; Kahrs 1998

Arthakriya (causal effectiveness): according to the Buddhist *Dharmakirti*, to exist is to be causally effective. Objective reality (*vastu*), independent of experiences, is defined as the capacity for being causally active. Only unique momentary particulars (*svalakshana*) are real and they are given only in immediate perceptual sensations. This criterion of reality rules out the existence of anything supposedly eternal and unchanging such as God, souls, the sounds of the Vedic scriptures, and primal material nature that is inert prior to its plural manifestation as the cosmos.

It appears that prior to *Dharmakirti* some of the *Abhidharma* thinkers applied the causal efficacy criterion of reality to conditioned, compound entities.

Dharmakirti's inference called *sattva-anumana* runs 'All realities are momentary, because existence consists in being causally effective. What is permanent has no causal functions (like a hare's horn) and is not real.' The use of the fictional example (obviously, there could not be a real one) invited the objection from realists, especially in the *Nyaya* school and their sympathisers, that the inference was invalid.

Further reading: Dunne 2004; Mookerjee 1975

Arthapatti (presumption): a form of inferential reasoning recognised as a reliable instrument of instrument of knowledge in its own right by *Kumarila*. Examples are: 'If fat Devadatta does not eat by day, he must eat by night'; 'If there were no persisting self that could anticipate the results of its actions, people would not act with view to future consequences.'

Further reading: Hiriyanna 1993; Suryanarayana Sastri 1942

Asatkaryavada ('production of something new'): the *Nyaya-Vaisheshika* theory of causation saying that, prior to origination, the effect did not exist in its underlying cause but is a totally new product, different from the already existent basic elements out of which it is made. They reject the category of potentiality, holding that only what is actual and concrete is real and can cause something else. Causation is not the actualisation of what was potential but the generation, through rearrangement, of new entities out of already existent factors. A cause is defined as a necessary prior condition of an effect. There are three factors in a causal complex: the underlying cause (*upadana* or *samavayi-karana*) which is always a type of substance (*dravya*), for example, the threads comprising the cloth (the new whole – *avayavin*); the non-inherent (*asamavayi*) which is always a quality (*guna*) or activity (*karman*), for example, the weaving and colour of the threads; the efficient or instrumental (*nimitta*), for example, the shuttle and other instruments. The weaver is the agent cause.

Reasons advanced for the view that, prior to origination, the effect does not exist in its underlying cause include:

1. The effect was not perceived in the causes.
2. If the pre-existent effect lacks specifiable properties, it is not identifiable and thus its existence does not fall within the province of inference.
3. The agent's efforts would be superfluous.
4. A pile of threads is not called 'cloth' and vice versa.
5. Difference in function: a lump of clay won't carry water.
6. Difference in form or shape.
7. Number: threads are many, the cloth one.

See *Karana, Satkaryavada*
Further reading: Halbfass 1992

Ashrama (stages of life): in mainstream orthodox Hinduism, the ideal life of a member of one of the three higher castes comprises four stages: celibate studentship (*brahmacarya*); householder (*grihastha*); forest dweller (*vanaprastha*); world renouncer (*samnyasin*). The householder is pivotal in the world of ordinary social relations. He generates wealth, provides for the family and pays for rituals that keep the world going. The practice of world renunciation (*samnyasa*) may have begun as the abdication of such responsibilities. (*Gautama* the *Buddha* and his followers are a case of men who have gone from home to homelessness.) Accordingly, orthodoxy accommodated renunciation by placing it at the end of life.

Further reading: Olivelle 1993

Asiddha-hetu (unestablished logical reason): one of the varieties of bogus reason (***hetvabhasa***) making an inference defective. It occurs when the logical reason does not occur in the subject (***paksha***) under consideration (*svarupa-asiddhi*); for example, 'sound is a property, because it is visible', and in cases where the subject of the inference does not exist or when its existence is controversial (*ashraya-asiddhi*). Buddhists apply this to what are held by Hindus to be proofs of the existence of the soul and its properties. They say that no soul is perceived apart from experiences, and, since it is the sort of thing that ought to be perceptible, its existence cannot be proved.

Further reading: G. Bhattacharya 1989; Potter and Bhattacharya 1993; Tillemans 1999

Atman (enduring soul/self): there is a widespread Hindu (and ***Jaina***) conviction that our experience of ourselves as the same individual is due to an unchanging non-physical and eternal factor over and above the stream of experiences making up embodied personality. The majority view is that the soul is neither known as an object, or in the ways in which objects are known. Objects need to be illuminated by something external, namely, consciousness, but the self-conscious soul is always directly aware of itself.

When the soul is subject to rebirth it is associated with a 'subtle body' consisting of residual impressions that are the good and bad *karma* produced by actions performed with some goal in view. It is the constant presence of the soul that guarantees the continuity of the same individual through a series of lives. Understanding the true nature of the soul is widely held to be a factor contributing to release from rebirth. Buddhists think that belief in its existence is at the root of human ills.

According to *Advaita Vedanta,* the *atman* is featureless, inactive awareness. It is self-evident and reveals itself in every conscious act. It is identical with *Brahman,* the foundational reality. Realisation of the unity of all souls means liberation from the series of births. For theistic *Vedanta,* souls are individual centres of self-awareness, the point of whose existence is the adoration of god (see *Ramanuja*). Both schools hold that soul may become misidentified with mind, body, and circumstances including one's caste. It may then be regarded as an agent who experiences the fruits of its actions. Release from rebirth involves the recovery and restoration of true identity.

According to *Nyaya-Vaisheshika,* souls are nonphysical and non-conscious principles of identity that explain our ability to remember and our capacity to synthesise the present variety of experiences into a unity. They are eternal and everywhere, though localisable in bodies. Thoughts, desires and acts of will cannot stand alone: there must be an enduring subject to which they belong. The existence of this non-mental principle of identity can only be known by inference. Not being conscious, it cannot make itself known. (Some *Nyaya* thinkers say that it

is perceptible by the inner sense (*manas*)
is experienced, this pleasure is a quality
self and cognition of a quality implies c
to which it belongs.) According to the
sakas, souls are eternal, conscious esser
erywhere. Their involvement in particular circumstances
and embodiment is due to *karma*. Permanent background
consciousness is constant amidst the variable psychological states brought about by interaction with the environment. Soul is known in the continuous experience of
subjectivity.

According to the *Samkhya* school, the souls are inactive
centres of consciousness, solitary witnesses uninvolved in
worldly life. The view that the soul is not essentially an
agent (agency being a function of embodiment) is characteristic of mainstream orthodox Brahminical traditions.
But all *Tantrics* hold that agency is intrinsic to the soul's
nature.

The *Carvaka* materialists say that soul is just the body
from which consciousness emerges as a by-product of
physical processes.

All forms of Buddhism deny the existence of an enduring soul, reducing personal identity to the interplay
of five impermanent constituents of personality (*skandhas*): matter, sensations, sense perceptions, behavioural
habits and thoughts. These components never amount to
an enduring, substantial self or soul. There is no 'inner
controller' that is the constant witness of experiences or
the persisting principle to which they are all related.

Further reading: Chakrabarti 1999; Lipner 1986;
Mookerjee 1975; Neevel 1977

Atma-guna: according to *Nyaya-Vaisheshika,* these are qualities specific to embodied souls. They are: cognitions (*jnana*), pleasures (*sukha*), pains (*duhkha*), desires

(*iccha*), antipathies (*dvesha*), deliberate effort (*prayatna*), spiritual merit (*dharma*) and demerit (*adharma*), and personality traits (*samskara*).

Further reading: G. Bhattacharya 1989; Matilal 1986

Atoms: in the Hindu **Vaisheshika** description of the cosmos, *atoms* (*anu/paramanu*) are the ultimately real raw material of the physical world. In the beginning, two form a pair, three pairs form a triplet, four triplets form a quadruplet and so on until there are entities of perceptible size (*dravya*) with persisting identities. The latter integrated wholes fall under natural kinds (*jati*, *samanya*).

The existence of imperceptible atoms is inferred. Every visible object has parts. Anything partite is further divisible. But division cannot continue indefinitely since every entity would consist of an infinity of parts and an elephant would be the same size as a mustard seed. So the process must halt, at which point we have the basic, uncaused *atoms*, of which the elephant has more than the mustard seed.

When a newly produced clay pot is heated in a furnace, its complex atomic structure disintegrates and each of its black earth-atoms turns red. One colour is replaced by another. There can be no change in the *atoms* which recombine to form a new pot. In this process, the *atoms* are the underlying, material cause, and the heat is the efficient cause. (The **Nyaya** school holds that the change of colour applies to the pot as a whole that is neither destroyed nor replaced by a new one.)

The Buddhist **Abhidharma** tradition posits types of mental and material *atoms* (*dharma*) with unchanging natures (*svabhava*) as the basic ingredients of all macroscopic and experiential processes. They alone are objectively real: anything made of parts exists by convention or manufacture.

Further reading: Frauwallner 1995; Halbfass 1992; Potter 1996

Avayavin (whole object): in contrast to the Buddhist reduction of what appear to be continuous objects to temporary collections of atomic factors and to the early *Samkhya* view that stable objects are just conglomerations of properties, the *Nyaya-Vaisheshika* school holds that persisting objects result from causal processes (*Asatkaryavada*) as integrated wholes. The whole is a new creation with its own identity, over and above the sum of the parts in which it inheres. The whole entity cannot exist without the parts, but the parts can exist without the whole. It is distinct from the parts since it manifests a single specific universal. An individual object must be the substrate of a universal, such as cowness or potness – a collection of different parts will not suffice. That the whole is not reducible to its parts is crucial to the *Nyaya-Vaisheshikas'* resistance to the Buddhist reduction of objects to constituents and phases. Endurance through space and time is explained in terms of integrated natures that are held together by inherence (*samavaya*). The continued existence of wholes requires that they retain all their parts over time. A partial replacement means the end of one whole and the generation of a new, similar one.

Further reading: Halbfass 1992

Avidya (ignorance): this has two senses: simple of lack of knowledge, and being wrong about something. In the first case, it is an absence but in the second it means a misconception that is mistaken for knowledge. Spiritual ignorance fuels the fires of rebirth. In many forms of Hinduism and Jainism, it condemns the eternal pure soul, its true nature lost from view, to a series of embodiments and, in Buddhism, propels the many streams of unsatisfactory existences saturated with greed and hatred. In early Buddhism, ignorance is usually of the *Four Noble Truths* and thus means a failure to appreciate the true nature of things as impermanent and lacking stable identities. The *Yoga* tradition classifies ignorance as a defect of the mind along with self-will, passion, hatred, obsessive attachments and instinctive drives.

The *Advaita Vedantin* philosopher *Shankara* says that ignorance is the same as the confusion (*adhyasa*) of what is subjective (the true self identical with the Absolute Reality or *Brahman*) and features of the objective world. This coupling of the true and false manifests itself in our habitual misguided practice of viewing body, mind, senses and will, which are not the self, as the true self. For him *avidya* is misconception and it is the nature of worldly existence. Later *Advaitins* treat it as a cosmic force (*bhava-rupa-avidya*) that is the material cause of all forms of misconception. This power of illusion is sometimes called *maya*.

The theistic Vedantin *Ramanuja* interprets ignorance as *karma* that obscures the soul's awareness of itself as God's servant. Kashmiri *Shaivas* belonging to the *Trika* cult understand ignorance, which they term *mala*, as oblivion of one's identity with the universal creative consciousness, and self-identification with one's human life in the world.

Further reading: Gethin 1998; Halbfass 1995; Lipner 1986; Rahula 1969

Bhagavad Gita ('Song of the Lord'): the *Gita* is a self-contained episode in a single book of the Sanskrit epic, the *Mahabharata*, one of whose principle themes is exploration of the tension between the life of activity in the world (*pravritti-dharma*) and the renunciation of society and organised religion (*nivritti-dharma*). The *Gita* was probably put together gradually in the two centuries before the Christian era. Within mainstream Hinduism, the *Gita* is classified as **smriti** (traditional teaching) that clarifies and supports the *Vedic* revelation. It is one of the basic authorities for **Vedanta**, and was the subject of commentaries by **Shankara, Ramanuja, Madhva** and their followers. Its synthesis of different paths (action, understanding and devotion to God) to salvation has opened it to many different interpretations.

A war is about to begin. *Arjuna* is in a chariot that is driven by the god *Krishna*. *Arjuna* is suddenly overcome by a crisis of conscience. How can he kill his relations and destroy the eternal laws of the family? He refuses to fight. *Krishna* tells him that warfare is his natural duty (*svadharma*) and it is better to perform one's own duty badly than that of another well. Human beings are immortal in that they have an everlasting and unchanging soul (*atman*). *Krishna* reveals that he is the god *Vishnu*, the creator, preserver, and destroyer of the worlds. His periodic 'descents' (*avatara*) restore righteousness (*dharma*) when it is in a state of decline. *Arjuna*'s dilemma illustrates the tension in orthodox Hinduism between duty and individual conscience, between self-determination and obedience to the rules derived from the infallible **Veda**. *Arjuna* is a member of the warrior caste (*varna*), one of whose natural duties and functions is warfare. We see the conflict between the values of non-violence (*ahimsa*) and what is ordained by the *Vedic* tradition. More generally, he represents those who renounce (*samnyasa*) their prescribed social and ritual duties and status in favour of a life of solitary homelessness, self-discipline and spiritual wisdom. Their goal is liberation (*moksha*) from rebirth, repetition, becoming and suffering (*samsara*). The active religion of the householder generating wealth, producing children and co-operating in the maintenance of social and cosmic order is inevitably involved in the sort of purposive action that binds one to *samsara* by generating *karma*. One of the questions that the *Gita* confronts is how one may continue to live in the world, obeying one's social and ritual duties, without generating *karma*. It rejects the path of radical renunciation and knowledge (*samnyasa*), teaching that, since action is unavoidable for embodied beings, one should renounce desire for the fruits of action, not actions themselves. Disinterested and disciplined action, action without a desire for its fruits, will not generate *karma*. This is called *karma-yoga*. The *Gita* is a monotheistic text and *Krishna* portrays himself as a creator god who has also ordained the social order. Since he is the source of all, the appropriate response is the dedication of actions and their results to him in a spirit of worship (*bhakti*). Moreover, God is the ultimate agent and humans merely instruments of what are in fact his actions. Realising that one is not really an agent and then performing all one's actions in service to God prompts saving divine grace (*prasada*) leading to liberation.

Further reading: Buitenen 1953; Johnson 1994; Lipner 1997; Matilal 2002a; Zaehner 1969

Bhakti-marga (path of devotion): a path to release from the series of rebirths whose critical component is devotion to God. Devotion may be a matter of passionate feeling but it may also be an attitude of mind – a lucid understanding of the natures of God and the soul in the light of which a person performs their social and religious obligations. This involves remembering that it is not just the person who acts but that God acts in them as the inner guide (*antaryamin*). Thus one acts not out of desire for the fruits of one's prescribed actions but in a spirit of awareness of God as the ultimate cause of one's very being.

Some devotional religions tend towards social inclusivity since anyone, be they high-caste Brahmins or outcastes, is capable of emotion. For this reason, it may be treated with suspicion by the orthodox.

Further reading: Hardy 1983

Bhartrihari (c. 430–80 CE): author of the *Vakyapadiya*, *Bhartrihari* was a Sanskrit grammarian who taught a version of philosophical monism. Whereas most non-dualistic (*Advaita*) philosophers identified the Absolute Reality (*Brahman*) with undifferentiated, static consciousness, *Bhartrihari* understood it as the undifferentiated essence of language (*shabda*) and meaning (*sphota*; 'the bursting forth of meaning). The Absolute-as-Meaning appears as many subjects, acts and objects of awareness in time and space through its principal autonomous power called time (*kala-shakti*). Meaning, although unitary, appears in sequences due to time. It appears to have parts because sound is differently manifested in time and space. Language and consciousness are inseparable, language being the creative 'vibration' in all awareness. *Bhartrihari* says that every cognition is saturated by words. If the identity of knowledge and words ceased, consciousness would not illuminate. It is this identity that makes reflective awareness possible.

Bhartrihari's basic insight in his theory of language is that the sentence is the basic linguistic fact and that individual words are grammarians' abstractions. Sentences and contexts, rather than individual words, are the actual vehicles of language. The primary linguistic fact is the sentence with an undivided meaning (*sphota*).

There are three stages of metaphysical and linguistic evolution from the undifferentiated 'Semantic-Absolute'.

The first principle from which the diverse universe emanates is called *pashyanti*: it is the pre-verbal stage of language at which it is identical with thought. There is an intermediate (*madhyama*) stage at which particular objects are separated but not yet identifiable. Language and thought are still one. Finally there is the physically manifested speech (*vaikhari*) that is the medium of worldly communication. The objects comprising the macroscopic world have become perceptible.

The dynamic supreme reality is manifested in kinds of being or universals that are the prototypes of particular beings. In this process, time is the regulatory power operating through the six modes of being and becoming (*bhava-vikara*). Due to the workings ignorance (*avidya*), another power of the Absolute, finite subjects of experience, whose consciousness is a reflection of that of the Absolute, fail to realise that the cosmic diversity is the self-manifestation of the Absolute and assume that the world exists in its own right. Once the unenlightened individual, which has misidentified itself with its embodied life, intuitively realises the identity of everything, including itself, with the Absolute, it is said to have achieved liberation from rebirth (*moksha*).

Further reading: Brough 1996a and 1996b; G. Shastri 1959

Bhaskara (c. 750 CE): a realist *Vedantin* commentator on the **Brahma-Sutras** and **Bhagavad Gita**, *Bhaskara* propounded a dualistic and theistic interpretation of the Hindu scriptures in opposition to non-dualist **Advaita-Vedanta**. He subscribed to the *satkaryavada* theory of causation according to which an effect pre-exists in its underlying cause before its manifestation as an entity with name and form. He understood the cosmos of souls and matter as the real rather than apparent transformation of one aspect of the Supreme Being (*Brahman*) that has become subject to limiting conditions (*upadhi*). The *Brahman* is both the underlying (*upadana-karana*) and instrumental (*nimitta-karana*) causes of the universe. His philosophy is called *bheda-abheda-vada* or the theory that the cosmos is differentiated while its source is unitary. Individual selves, subject to restricted awareness, the workings of *karma* and rebirth are emanations of the Supreme Being. They are comparable to sparks from fire. In defence of his position against the charge that conditioning by limits introduces imperfection into the godhead, *Bhaskara* uses a simile: just as atmosphere contained in a jar is different from the whole atmosphere in that the former is limited and the latter unrestricted and unconnected with the properties in the jar, similarly, defects occurrent in the embodied soul, differentiated and conditioned by limiting adjuncts, do not really affect the *Brahman*.

Against non-dualist *Vedanta* he argues that if the world of differences and agency are just products of beginningless, primal ignorance (*avidya*), then we have no grounds for thinking that monistic belief is true since it too occurs in the sphere of *avidya*.

The individual souls' desires for worldly things causes their bondage to rebirth. Transformation of desire into devotional meditation (*bhakti*) upon the Supreme Being brings about liberation. The agency of the embodied soul is real, although 'borrowed' from *Brahman*, its ultimate source. Against the renunciatory (*samnyasa*) outlook characteristic of *Advaita-Vedanta*, *Bhaskara* holds that the scripturally prescribed duties (*dharma*) appropriate to caste and stage of life always apply. Performance of ritual duties combined with understanding of the natures of the soul and **Brahman** as the source of all is necessary for salvation.

Further reading: Rocher 1988

Bhava-rupa-avidya (misconception as a positive force): *Advaita Vedantins* such as **Prakashatman,** *Vimuktatman* and *Sarvajnatman* hold that there is a force called positive ignorance that projects the appearance of diversification into individual agents and objects of experience and conceals the nature of the Absolute Reality that they understand as inactive, featureless consciousness. Positive ignorance is removed by knowledge, is beginningless, and is a positive reality. It differs from the sort of ignorance that is the absence of knowledge of an object prior to its apprehension.

Bhava-vikara (modes of being and becoming): these apply to material objects and are origination, continuing existence, growth, change in properties, decay and destruction. The soul (*atman*) is exempt from them.

Bheda-abheda-vada: *Bhaskara* and *Yadavaprakasha* thought that the world was a real transformation out of the Supreme Being (*Brahma-parinama-vada*). If this process is regarded as a transformation of the real nature of the godhead, it looks as if it is becoming less than perfect. For this reason **Ramanuja** replaces the theory that the world is a real modification of God (*Brahma-parinama-vada*) with the idea that the relation between God and the world should be understood on the model of the relationship between the individual soul and its body. Bodies are essentially dependent entities really distinct from souls. Since the manifestation of the cosmos is a modification of God's body (*Brahma-sharira-parinama-vada*), his perfection is preserved.

Further reading: Bartley 2002; Buitenen 1956; Lipner 1986

Brahma-Sutras: a collection of very brief summaries (*sutra*), intended as aids to memory, of the main teachings of the Hindu scriptures called *Upanishads*. The collection is ascribed to *Badarayana* and was probably composed around the beginning of the common era. With the *Upanishads* and *Bhagavad Gita*, they form the triple basis of the *Vedanta* school of scriptural interpretation. Any thinker who wanted to be recognised as a *Vedantin* had to write a commentary explaining these pithy and ambiguous statements. The earliest surviving commentary on the *Brahma-Sutras* is that by the non-dualist (*Advaita*) *Vedantin Shankara* (700–50 CE). The theistic theologian *Ramanuja*'s commentary is called the *Shri Bhashya*.

Brahman: the *Vedantic* term meaning 'Supreme Being'. *Advaita* understands it as an impersonal absolute beyond all oppositions, not a creator. It is just static awareness, void of differentiating features, the substratum of the false appearance of diversity. Although this *Brahman* is beyond thought and language, scriptural texts expressing identity can point us in the right direction (see *Neti Neti*).

In *Ramanuja*'s theistic *Vedanta*, the Supreme Being is the personal God *Vishnu-Narayana* who is the originating and sustaining cause of the cosmos to which he is related in the way in which individual souls are related to their bodies. This maximally great and good deity comprises an infinity of delightful unsurpassable qualities. Its producing and holding in existence the cosmos is a tiny feature of the divine life. Scripture (*shruti*) describes *Brahman* as the originating and sustaining cause of the cosmos, but this is not the definition (*lakshanam*) of the term. The definition is, 'The Supreme Being is reality, consciousness, infinite', which both ascribes essential properties and distinguishes *Brahman* from contingent and finite beings.

Further reading: Bartley 2002; Lipner 1986

Buddhi (intellectual faculty): the *Samkhya-Yoga*, *Vedanta*, *Pratyabhijna* and *Shaiva-Siddhanta* philosophical schools use the term *buddhi* (or *antah karana* – inner sense) for the psychological faculty whose modifications (*vritti*) are our thoughts and feelings. It is an emergent product of primal material nature (*prakriti*) that becomes conscious when irradiated by the consciousness that belongs to the soul (*atman*) that has become associated with a body. The combination of the light of consciousness and the activity of the intellect contributes to the formation of individual embodied personality. The operations of the *buddhi* are our internal mental life. As a composite of matter and consciousness it mediates between the inner spiritual essence and the material environment.

Anti-Buddhist thinkers differentiate transitory mental events comprising a stream of consciousness from the constant soul. They distinguish transient psychological episodes (*buddhi-vritti*) whose nature is definite awareness perception (*adhyavasaya*) from permanent background subjective awareness (*samvid*) of whose beginning and end we have no experience. The former are variable because they occur in the essentially material and mutable mind. The latter is the constant awareness (*samvedana*) of oneself as the same subject of experience, and it is a constitutive feature of the human condition.

Further reading: Goodall 1998; Hiriyanna 1993; Larson and Bhattacharya 1987; Mayeda 1979; Torella 2002

C

Carvaka: Indian atheistic and anti-ritualist outlook holding that sensory perception (*pratyaksha*) is the only authoritative method of obtaining knowledge (*pramana*). They reject inference (*anumana*), as a *pramana* in its own right because the limited range of human observations can never guarantee conclusions that are both general and true.

The *Carvakas* recognise the existence of the four material elements: earth, fire, air and water. They deny the soul (*atman*) and say that personal identity is just bodily continuity. Consciousness emerges from physical processes. Feelings are identical with their bodily expressions. The decomposition after death of the body is the absolute and final dissolution of the self.

Of the four legitimate goals of life (*purusartha*), they recognise only economic prosperity (*artha*) and aesthetic and sexual enjoyment (*kama*), and reject social and religious duty (*dharma*) and final release from the series of births (*moksha*). They propose a mild hedonism: 'enjoy yourself while you are alive'. *Carvakas* reject the morally retributive **karma** theory since they think that the relation of cause and effect is restricted to what is natural and observable.

Further reading: Cowell and Gough 1996; Franco 1994

Caste (*Varna*): the Brahminical Hindu system of the hierarchical classification of the human world into four kinds of beings: *Brahmins* who are intellectuals and priests; *Kshatriyas*, warriors and rulers; *Vaishyas*, farmers and merchants; *Shudras* who provide various services to members of the higher three estates. Only members of the first three estates, who are termed 'twice-born' because they have undergone the caste initiation ceremony (*upanayana*) entitling them to wear the sacred thread, have the qualification (*adhikara*) to participate in the *Vedic* ritual religion. But in addition to the members of the lowest *Shudra-varna* there is the remainder of the population who are classified as 'outcaste' or 'untouchable'. Each estate, as well as the outcastes, consists of *jatis* that are the actual units of social organisation. Ideally you should only marry someone belonging to your own *jati*. *Jatis* are tied to hereditary trades and professions, thus effectively guaranteeing employment for those born into them. While inequality is essential to the system, the hierarchical arrangement is cohesive rather than divisive. *Jatis* are interdependent; that is to say, in a non-monetary economy, a *Brahmin* might provide religious offices in exchange for goods and other services.

Jatis are natural kinds of beings: the word can mean 'birth' or 'biological species', as well as hereditary social grouping. It follows that there is no concept of humanity. Birth into a particular *jati* is determined by the quality of one's *karma:* the accumulated consequences of good and bad deeds performed in an infinite series of past lives. The hierarchy is ordered by considerations of spiritual purity. *Brahmins* keep their status at the top by strictly observing a vast catalogue of rules set down in the **Dharma Shastras**. These rules apply to every aspect of life, and isolate the pure (*shuddha*) from the spiritually polluting or impure forces that are everywhere. The maintenance of purity involves keeping the company of other *Brahmins*, studying the *Vedic* literature, various daily and occasional religious rituals, and the avoidance of polluting physical contact with members of lower castes as far as possible.

Further reading: Dumont 1980; Sanderson 1985

Darshana (philosophical outlook/system): this is a term applied to what Hindu *Brahmin* intellectuals consider to be the six orthodox systems of philosophy and paths to ultimate human well-being. They are *Nyaya* and *Vaisheshika*, *Samkhya* and *Yoga*, *Purva Mimamsa* and *Vedanta*.

Dharma (natural law/social and religious duty): a fundamental Brahminical Hindu concept, *dharma* is revealed by the infallible **Vedas**. It is the *dharma* of grass to grow and of the sun to shine. It is the *dharma* of members of the Brahmin **caste** to study and teach the **Veda** and the *dharma* of *Vaishyas* to engage in agriculture or commerce. *Dharma* would be unknown were it not taught by the **Veda**. This ethic is thoroughly deontological. Consequentialist standards such as welfare, pleasure and pain, the biddings of conscience, divine command or the cultivation of virtuous character are all irrelevant to the determination of what is right and wrong. Values are exclusively defined by Vedic injunctions and prohibitions, and are manifested in the 'conduct of the virtuous' that derives from strict observance of the Vedic rules separating the pure from the pollutant.

Initially, the observance of *dharma* chiefly involved the performance and patronage of elaborate and expensive rituals generating prosperity (*bhoga*) and temporary enjoyments in a heaven (*svarga*). Its neglect has all sorts of negative consequences ranging from personal misfortunes to the collapse of the universe into chaos.

For the later *Purva Mimamsaka* theorists of ritual and social duty, the accurate performance of both the public rituals by Brahmin priests and the domestic rituals by householders of the highest three *castes*, in addition to observance of the obligations appropriate to one's *caste* and stage of life controls, maintains and perpetuates order and stability in the universe. A properly performed rite automatically produces its result. It does not depend upon a god. To account for cases where the rite is not observed to deliver its promised result, the *Mimamsakas* introduced a special form of supernatural causal power (*apurva*) belonging to properly performed ritual acts that brings about their results in the future.

Dharma is not a 'universal' ethic because its demands vary according to one's caste and stage of life. One and the same type of action might be right for one person (*sva-dharma* = 'own *dharma*') and wrong for another. There was a widespread recognition of the principle that it is better to perform one's own *dharma* badly than that of another well.

See *Ahimsa*

Further reading: Halbfass 1991; Olivelle 1999; Sanderson 1985

Dharmakirti (600–60 CE): major Buddhist philosopher who agrees with *Dignaga* that objective reality is a flux of momentary unique particulars (*svalakshana*) that are inexpressible and incommunicable as such. Each has its own causal effectiveness (*arthakriya*). To be is to be causally effective. Each particular has specific location, time and form.

The *svalakshanas* are given in sensory perception (*pratyaksha*), which he defines as awareness that is free from concepts and that is reliable (*abhranta*). Sensory impressions are copied by images that are interpreted in concepts by a mind conditioned by its past experiences (*vasana*). So the external unique particulars are the indirect objects of thoughts. The unique instants behave in such a way that we can organise them under unifying concepts. While our concepts, involving the association of names and general properties with the given, do not copy the fluid play of the real particulars, they represent it indirectly. We cannot directly know reality as it is in itself because we are primarily aware of images derived form sensory impressions.

Dharmakirti says that the activity of conceptual construction (*kalpana*) is cognition involving a representation that is capable of being expressed in words. Once an aspect of reality has been mentally discriminated (*adhyavasaya*), we can act in relation to it. Sense perception on its own has no practical application because it does not discriminate anything. Judgements using concepts lead to successful activity when they are causally related to real particulars. But it is a natural mistake to suppose that our concepts are copies of reality. Error occurs when we think that our representations stand for reality as it is in itself.

See **grahya-grahaka-vibhaga**

Further reading: Dunne 2004; Kajiyama 1998; Mookerjee 1975; Prasad 2002; Stcherbatsky 1993; Tillemans 1999

Dharmakirti on perception: *Dharmakirti* says that true cognition is the presupposition of all successful human activity. The reliable means of knowledge (*pramana*) is true cognition relating to an object not already known. It is twofold: direct perception and inference. Perception is free from conceptualisation (*kalpana*) and is reliable (*abhranta*). He rejects *Dignaga*'s view that thought and language always go together and claims that thought is prior to language: conceptualisation is a cognition involving a representation (*pratibhasa*) that is *capable* of linguistic expression.

Perception is fourfold: sensory impressions; a mental image produced from the sensory impressions that are its immediately preceding cause; the self-awareness of every thought and feeling; yogic awareness produced by contemplative insight into the truth. Perception relates to the unique, momentary particulars (*svalakshana*). They alone are objectively real because reality means the capacity for causal effectiveness (*arthakriya*). Generalising conceptualisation (*samanya-lakshana*) is distanced from the unique instants and is a type of inference. Sensory awareness leads to knowledge when it is truly related to the object. Sensation of a blue object (that is, impressions derived from unique particulars which have the power to produce the experience of blue) produces a dual awareness comprising a blue mental image (*akara*) and consciousness of the blue mental image. The image copies the impressions and the constructive mind, conditioned by traces of prior experiences (*vasana*), interprets the image by applying a concept (*vikalpa*) that enables us to think, act and communicate. While some complex concepts ultimately derive from sensory impressions and mental images formed from them, others, including those of the persisting soul and real cause–effect relations, are produced by the creative imagination.

Realists, such as followers of **Nyaya** and **Vaisheshika**, make the mistake of supposing that our conceptual schemes are direct copies of objectively real structures and entities.

See *adhyavasaya*

Further reading: Dunne 2004; Kajiyama 1998; Mookerjee 1975

Dharma Shastras: catalogues of rules delineating a pure way of life for Hindus who understand themselves as following the orthodox *Vedic* tradition. They offer an exhaustive and detailed specification of right actions for members of the different castes (although the law books are chiefly concerned with the obligations of Brahmins).

The conduct of every aspect of life is rule governed. Conformity to *dharma* through the performance of ritual and social duties prevents pollution by contaminating forces, and its neglect generates bad *karma*.

Further reading: Olivelle 1999; O'Flaherty 1991

Dignaga (480–540 CE): Buddhist philosopher whose most important work is the *Pramana-samuccaya*.

Dignaga radically divorces sensory perception and thought involving concepts and words (which, using the word in a broad sense, he calls inference). Sensory perception never involves conceptualisation. Perception is direct experience of objective reality, which consists of a flux of unique, momentary particulars (*svalakshana*). Because they do not share any common features, they are indescribable. The categories (*padartha*) that the *Nyaya-Vaisheshika* realists claim to find in the world are imposed by our minds.

Conceptual thought (*kalpana*) and language deal in generalities (*samanya-lakshana*). Even simple concepts are at one remove from reality because there are no objective general features. They are, however, causally related to the realities and not just arbitrary fictional inventions. But there is a gap between how our minds work and the way things are. The map is not the territory. Thought and language are inseparable: conceptual thought is born out of language and language is born out of concepts. Conceptual construction is the interpretation of what is given by sensory impressions via proper names, words for general features (*jati, samanya*), words for qualities (*guna*), words for actions (*karman*) and words for individual substances (*dravya*). Our minds group unique particulars together and we understand them as continuing objects bearing types of properties.

He inherits the terms *svalakshana* and *samanya-lakshana* from the *Abhidharma* tradition. There *svalakshana* refers to an individual basic atomic factor (*dharma*) as it is in itself and *samanya-lakshana* means the features common to *dharmas* when their combinations produce conditioned, macroscopic formations. Such generalities include non-eternity, unsatisfactoriness and lack of permanent identity. He models the notion of the unique instantaneous particular (*svalakshana*) on the *Abhidharma* notion of *dharma*, but he rejects their view that each atomic factor has an unchanging essence.

His contribution to the theory of inference was considerable (see *Trairupya-hetu*). He insisted that all inferential thought occurred at a remove from reality: 'All this convention involving inferential reason and properties to be established is based on the distinction between property and property-possessor which is itself a feature of the human mind: it is not grounded in anything existing outside the mind.'

See *Alambana, Apoha-vada, Dharmakirti*

Further reading: Ganeri 2001a; Hattori 1968; Hayes 1988; Matilal 1986; Mookerjee 1975; Oetke 1994

Dravya (continuing object or substance): one of the types of objectively real basic features (*padartha*) of the cosmos according to the *Vaisheshikas*. *Dravyas* are persistently enduring objects with constant natures that possess persisting qualities and transitory motions. Substance is defined as that which lacks the constant absence of qualities and motions. They are not properties of anything else. At the moment of origination, substances lack qualities and motions but the object has an identity in that it belongs to a kind, is the locus of a universal and has a form. A substance or basic particular is a subject distinct from its properties rather than just a confluence of properties. The category includes the different types of irreducible and indestructible atoms comprising the elements (earth, water, fire and air); the atmosphere (the vehicle of sounds), time, space (which are unitary and all-pervasive); and also souls (*atman*) and the inner sense (*manas*).

Atoms are the raw material of the cosmos. They combine to form the perceptible objects that are the furniture of our world. Substances are individuated by the different arrangements of their parts.

A substance is an integrated whole (*avayavin*) product that comes into being as a novel unit, over and above the sum of its parts. The whole cannot exist without the parts in which it inheres (*samavaya*).

One argument in favour of the existence of complex objects with natures that remain stable through time is that an entity may be simultaneously seen and touched. But each sensory quality is apprehensible only through the corresponding sense organ. So what is knowable by more than one sense must be other than the sensible qualities. This object of synthetic perception must be the form of an integrated whole entity.

Further reading: G. Bhattacharya 1989; Halbfass 1992; Potter 1977

Drishtanta (example): in an inference (*anumana*), the general principle being appealed to needs to be supported by examples.

See *Hetu*, *Sapaksha* and *Vipaksha*

Drishya-anupalabdhi (non-cognition of the knowable): according to *Dharmakirti*, the non-apprehension of an entity that is of a perceptible kind proves the absence of that entity. This principle is applied in arguments with those who believe that we are fundamentally souls (*atman*). The characterisations of the soul that are proposed imply that it is the sort of thing that should be uncontroversially knowable. *Dharmakirti* and other Buddhists focus on the problems of disentangling the soul from the personality and its experiences. They reason that it is never known, although it is described as the sort of thing that is knowable. This non-apprehension proves its non-existence.

The same pattern of reasoning is applied to the notion of Prime Matter (*prakriti*), which is supposed by *Samkhyas* and *Vedantins* to be the ultimate source and underlying cause of all material products.

But the fact that we do not see supernatural entities, such as ghosts, does not prove that they do not exist because they are by nature inaccessible to normal perception. This applies to anything inaccessible to perception by virtue of space, time or nature. This is applied in arguments about the existence of other minds. From the fact that we do not perceive them it does not follow that they do not exist.

See *Anupalabdhi-hetu*

Further reading: Kajiyama 1998; Tillemans 1999; Wood 1991

Duhkha (suffering, frustration, unsatisfactoriness): agreed by almost everyone to characterise transmigratory existence (*samsara*) or the series of embodied lives in the here and now. It is one of the basic truths discovered by the Buddha that everything is *duhkha*, impermanent and devoid of unchanging identity (*anatta*). This means more than the fact that life is sometimes sad and that toothache is unpleasant. It is obvious that not all experiences are painful. Rather, it expresses the view that human projects, however noble their aspirations, end in failure and disappointment. It is the outlook of the person who has examined all the sources of consolation and found them wanting. Buddhism says one of our basic problems is a selfish thirst for more experiences, more lives. Life has proved unsatisfactory, so we want more of it in the hope that it will get better. The subjective experiences of discontent, frustration and disappointment happen because we cling to what is by nature impermanent.

Further reading: Collins 1982; Conze 1959; Gethin 1998; Williams 1998

Dvaita-Vedanta: a strongly dualistic school expressing a rigorously monotheistic *Vishnu* cult, this tradition was inaugurated in South West India in the thirteenth century by *Madhva* in reaction to the ultimately anti-theistic nondualism of *Advaita-vedanta* and as a response to the *Vishishta-advaita* of *Ramanuja* whose intimate association of God and the essentially dependent soul he regarded as compromising God's transcendent perfection. He departed from the tenets of mainstream *Vedanta* by denying that God is both the material and the efficient causes of the world. God creates by organising an independent material principle subject to his governance. Other exponents are the acute logicians *Jayatirtha* (1345–88) and *Vyasatirtha* (1460–1539), both of whom commented on *Madhva*'s expositions of the *Upanishads*, *Bhagavad Gita* and *Brahma Sutras*.

Dvaitins uphold the existence of a plurality of individual selves and the mind-independence of the physical world, both of which are existentially dependent upon *Vishnu* who is the only truly independent and self-sufficient reality that sustains everything. Devotion (*bhakti*) to the personal deity leads to release from rebirth.

Every entity intrinsically possesses a distinguishing feature (*vishesha*) that identifies it uniquely. We immediately know entities, and ourselves, in their uniqueness without having to compare them with anything else.

The universe is structured in terms of five types of real difference: the difference between God (*Vishnu*) and the individual soul, that between material objects and God, differences between individual souls, differences between individual souls and material objects, and differences between material objects. This universe is real and has no beginning. If it began, it would end. But it does not end. It is not imaginatively constructed due to misconception. Were it imagined, it would cease. But it does not cease. The *Advaitins* are mistaken in thinking that difference is unreal. Plurality is sustained and known by *Vishnu* and so it is real.

Further reading: Betty 1978; Gerow 1990; Sarma 2003; Sharma 1986

Four Buddhist schools: the *Vaibhashikas* believe that we directly perceive objects outside the mind by the senses; the *Sautrantikas* say that we only infer the existence of mind-independent realities on the basis that different representative ideas figure in consciousness; the *Vijnanavadins* (*Yogacara*) deny that there are any physical objects outside consciousness and the *Madhyamikas* say that there are no unchanging essential natures and that there can be no complete and correct theories about what there is.

Four Noble Truths: the basic principles of the universal system of belief thought by Buddhists to have been discovered by *Siddhartha Gotama* (*Shakyamuni*), called the *Buddha* or 'Enlightened One' (c. 450–400 BCE).

Buddhists believe that the basic source of human discontent (*duhkha*) is a mistaken belief that one is an enduring single entity with a fixed identity – in short, a soul (*atman*). This mistaken perspective on life generates selfishness, attachments, fearful hostility to whatever we think poses a threat to our personal wants, and a thirst for more experiences, which we can call our own. They deny that anything made of parts is ultimately real. Basic realities are in a state of ceaseless change (*Kshanikatva*). There are no permanent identities and thus no real distinction between enduring entities and their properties. Reality is basically an impersonal process.

The truths are:

1. All compounded and conditioned things are ultimately unsatisfactory (*Duhkha/Dukkha*). This is the eternal round of existences (*samsara*). A mode of existence is determined by the quality of the accumulated *karma* in a stream of experiences that temporarily forms a succession of lives.

   Universal unsatisfactoriness is attributed to the impermanence (*anitya*; *anicca*) and non-substantiality (*anatma*; *anatta*) of all conditioned entities. Buddhism propounds anti-essentialist and reductionist theories in its process or event ontologies. What appear to be stable and integral spatio-temporal continuants are reduced to temporary parts; human lives are analysed into streams of causally interdependent psychophysical components (*skandhas*) that do not amount to an enduring, substantial self or soul. Selfhood is a fiction that the fluxes of experiences conventionally called persons superimpose upon themselves. Attempts to cling to what is unstable and impermanent are bound to end in disappointed frustration.

2. The second truth discovered by the Buddha is that there is a causal explanation (*pratitya-samutpada*) for the arising of unsatisfactoriness in terms of 'thirst', which

serves as a metaphor for desire and attachment, and ignorance of the way things really are as expressed in the four noble truths. Unenlightened actions are motivated by craving or aversion or delusion.

3. There is potentially an end to *duhkha*, called *Nirvana* or *Nibbana*. This is the end of the series of unsatisfactory existences through the extinction of the fires of craving, hatred and delusion that generate rebirth-causing actions.

4. There is a path to the cessation of *duhkha* (*Noble Eightfold Path*).

Further reading: Bechert and Gombrich 1984; Collins 1982; Conze 1959; Gethin 1998; Rahula 1969

$$\boxed{\text{G}}$$

Gaudapada (450–500 CE): an early non-dualist *Advaita Vedantin*, *Gaudapada* was the author of the *Agama-Shastra*, also known as the *Gaudapada-Karikas* or *Mandukya-Karikas*. Although a *Vedantin*, he was clearly influenced by the Buddhist philosopher *Nagarjuna* and the Buddhist idealist *Vasubandhu*.

He contends that objects seen in dreams are unreal. But so are ones seen when awake because they too come and go, while only consciousness remains constant. If entities are unreal, how do they arise? The Supreme Soul imagines itself as the individual soul. Then it imaginatively creates what become the differentiated contents of the individual's experiences.

Nothing is really originated because only consciousness, or the Supreme Soul, exists and it has neither beginning nor end. Nothing can be really produced because that would mean that it did not exist before. And nothing comes from nothing. But if something existed already, it would not need to be produced. So there are no individuals apart from the Supreme Soul and its inventions

When the mind withdraws from the objects of experience to which it has become attached, its tranquillity is restored. Renunciation (*samnyasa*) of normal society and religion follows the realisation that everything other than consciousness is unreal. Profound meditation reveals the identity of the individual and supreme souls.

Further reading: Karmarkar 1953; King 1995; Potter 1981

God's existence see *Ishvara*

Grahya-grahaka-vibhaga (percept–perceiver/grasper–grasped dichotomy): for Buddhists in the tradition of *Dignaga* and *Dharmakirti,* the oppositions between the perceiving subject, objects and thoughts are human inventions and not objective realties. Awareness is uniform but due to mistaken views it appears differentiated. It is we who contrast subjects and objects, thinking them external to each other. The appearance of oppositions between subjects, acts and objects of cognition within the one reality arises from different influences (*vasana*) of previous ideas in a beginningless and uninterrupted stream of experiences. Positing oneself as an individual thinker facing a world of objects is a kind of selfishness that Buddhist practice aims to eliminate. One way to do this is to adopt the attitude that there are only experiences, but no personal individuality. Since the polar notions of object and subject are interdependent, by exposing the falsity of one, we can expose the falsity of the other. Once a person has really understood that the conventional view of reality as objective and mind independent is false and that our thoughts do not copy whatever objective reality may be, they also understand that subjectivity and its attachments is an illusory construct.

Guna (quality-particular, trope): one of the *Vaisheshika* basic categories of reality (*padartha*), these are permanent characteristics of enduring objects (*dravya*) and cannot stand alone. They are other than enduring substances and motions. They fall under real universals. Some are physical features: colours, tastes, smells, touch, sounds (each exclusively related to the appropriate sense organ); proximity, distance, gravity, liquidity, viscidity and dimension. Others are non-physical properties specific to embodied selves: cognitions, pleasures, pains, desires, antipathies, conscious efforts, spiritual merit and demerit, and dispositions of personality. All of those listed so far occur as properties specific to each individual substance but we also find number, severalty, conjunction and disjunction, which always apply to a plurality of distinct individual substances.

Gunas are unique particular occurrences (sometimes called 'tropes'). The red specific to my table is a different instance from the red specific to my tie, although the two shades may be identical. Redness is not a quality but the universal (*samanya*) common to all instances of red. Since a colour pervades the whole substance in which it inheres, seeing an object's colour implies seeing the entire object.

The *Nyaya-Vaisheshikas* infer the existence of the non-perceptible and in itself non-conscious soul on the grounds that cognitions, desires and effort are qualities and as such require a substrate to which they belong.

The *Purva Mimamsakas* treat *gunas* as universals, saying that they are eternal, unitary and present in many individuals. All red individuals are instances of the singular property redness. A persisting object may undergo changes in its qualities while retaining its essential identity.

Further reading: G. Bhattacharya 1989; Halbfass 1992

Guna (strand): according to the *Samkhya* system, primal material nature (*pradhana* or *mula-prakriti*) comprises three strands or *gunas*: *sattva* (goodness and light), *rajas* (dynamic energy) and *tamas* (heavy and dark). Prior to the emergence of the differentiated cosmos from material, the *gunas* are in a state of equilibrium, cancelling out each other's specific characteristics. But, once the process of cosmic emergence begins, the balance is upset and they occur in different relative preponderances in the material entities produced from *prakriti*, including our bodies and mental apparatus.

Further reading: Larson 1979; Larson and Bhattacharya 1987

Hetu: the logical reason in an inference (*anumana*). When we infer the presence of fire on a mountain from the observation of smoke, smoke is the reason. We must know that the reason is invariably accompanied (*vyapti*) by the object to be inferred (*sadhya*). It occurs wherever the *sadhya* occurs. This knowledge may be expressed by an agreeing example (*sapaksha, sadharmya-drishtanta*): 'where there's smoke, there's fire; as in the kitchen', and a disagreeing example (*vipaksha, vaidharmya-drishtanta*): 'where there's no fire, there's no smoke; as in a lake'. Such a dual instance is called 'invariable concomitance supported by agreement and difference' (*anvaya-vyatireka-vyapti*).

The reason is 'only agreeing' (***kevala-anvayi***) in an inference such as, 'The pot is nameable because it is knowable'. Since every entity is knowable and nameable, there can be no negative instance.

The reason is 'only disagreeing' (***kevala-vyatireki***) in an inference such as, 'Living bodies have souls, since they are animate'. There can be no positive example (*sapaksha*) apart from the subject of the inference (living bodies), so the negative instance, 'unlike a pot' (which instances the invariant association of lack of soul and insentience), must suffice. (See ***Ishvara, proving the existence of God***, for another example.)

Further reading: G. Bhattacharya 1989; Ganeri 2001a; Ganeri 2001b; Kajiyama 1998; Matilal 1998; Oetke 1994

Hetvabhasa (logical fallacy): literally, fake, merely apparent or bogus reason in an inference. As is to be expected, the precise number and character of these is a matter of controversy.

See ***Anaikantika-hetu, Asiddha-hetu, Viruddha-hetu***

Further reading: Potter 1977; Potter and Bhattacharya 1993

Iccha (will, desire): *Nyaya-Vaisheshika* classifies willing or wanting as one of the qualities (***guna***) specific to souls (***atman***). Qualities require a substrate. The occurrence of acts of will inferentially establishes the existence of a continuous principle of identity (the *Nyaya* denies that the non-conscious soul is knowable through introspection). It is wanting something seen that inclines us to act in one way or another. Will becomes effort (*yatna* or *kriti*) whence follows action. Wanting is connected with pleasures and pains, which are also categorised as qualities of the soul, but these are best understood as unconscious drives rather than conscious experiences. *Utpaladeva* and *Abhinavagupta* understand *iccha* as precognitive impulse. With knowledge and action, it is a power (*shakti*) belonging to the universal dynamic and creative consciousness that excites it to project the subjects, objects and acts of experience that make up the cosmos.

Further reading: G. Bhattacharya 1989; Matilal 1986; Potter 1977

Indriya (the sense faculties): according to the *Samkhya* system, the five senses are amongst the physical faculties that evolve from primal matter (*prakriti*). The senses grasp data about objects which they transmit to the intellect (*buddhi*), which interprets that sensory information and forms ideas about what is presented. These ideas are observed by the conscious soul, which remains unmodified by its embodied experiences. All *Vedantins* share this outlook.

The *Nyaya-Vaisheshikas* say that a perception (*pratyaksha*) is a cognitive episode (*jnana*) that is produced by a form of contact between the physical sense faculties and the colours, shapes, sounds, smells and tastes of external objects to which each is related. Their account of the psychology of perception is basically a physical one. The senses grasp the object and transduce information about it to the coordinating faculty (*manas*), which is also physical. The *manas*, the central processor, operates on the information received, which may be converted into a cognition that is raised to the level of explicit awareness. A cognition occurs in the principle of identity (*atman*). Whether the information becomes conscious awareness is determined by what is relevant to the present state of the complex of experiences that is unified by being related to the one identity. This account of perceptual process explains why I can say that I am touching and tasting what I also see. Although each sense is correlated with its proper objects, the *manas* synthesises the information received.

The dominant Buddhist outlook is that each sense-faculty is exclusively correlated with its proper objects, each sense-object contact producing a different type of awareness. So when the eye, for example, is related to colours and shapes, a visual sensation occurs and it produces a visual awareness. But they have a problem in that they admit neither a persisting mind nor a persisting subject of experience. Instead, different sensory impressions naturally cooperate to produce a complex sensation in a stream of experiences.

Further reading: G. Bhattacharya 1989; Chakrabarti 1999; Larson and Bhattacharya 1987; Potter 1977; Stcherbatsky 1993

Ishvara, proving the existence of God: given assumptions that the existence of the world is not self-explanatory and that its organisation cannot be accounted for by unconscious factors like *karma*, some *Nyaya* thinkers try to prove inferentially the existence of the unperceived God by considering aspects of the world which imply a creator capable of planning.

Vacaspati Mishra (850 or 976 CE) argues that we know that some objects have makers, while realities such as the atmosphere do not. But we do not know whether many natural phenomena such as mountains, oceans and the earth itself have makers or not. Assuming, on the basis of reason and repeated observations, that whatever consists of parts is a product and that things such as pots do not occur spontaneously, the inference runs:

> Mountains etc. (*paksha*) have an intelligent and powerful creator (*sadhya* or property to be proved)
> Because they are products (*hetu* or logical reason)
> Whatever is a product has an intelligent maker (*vyapti*- invariable association) – like pots
> Mountains etc. are products
> So they have an intelligent and powerful creator.

Another argument is:

> The complex cosmos has an intelligent maker, because it has a particular organisation of its parts. Whatever has a particular organisation of its parts has an intelligent maker. Whatever does not have an intelligent maker lacks organisation of parts, like atoms and space.

(This is an example of the 'only negative' (*kevala-vyatireka*) type of inference. The worry is that the positive formulation 'Whatever has a particular organisation of its parts has an intelligent maker; like a pot' would prove a finite creator. *See hetu.*)

The invariant association here is a general one between complexity and creation by intelligence. The next step is to argue that nothing is a product of *intelligent cause in general*, and, considering the nature of the world, it must have a specific type of cause that is all-knowing and all-powerful.

Vedantic theologians such as **Ramanuja** deny that the existence of the Supreme Being can be proved by inference and appeal only to the scriptures. *Ramanuja* argues that, even granting that diverse natural phenomena are products, there is no reason to suppose that they were made by one creator at one time. If anything, the differences in their natures suggest that they have different makers. Even if it is true that every product presupposes a maker, it does not follow that there is a single creator of every product.

Further reading: Chemparathy 1972; Clooney 2001; Potter and Bhattacharya 1993; Thibaut 1904a; Vattanky 1984

J

Jaina doctrines: the cosmos comprises an infinity of individual souls and what is inanimate. There is no creator God involved with the world.

There are six types of substances (*dravya*): eternal souls, movement and stability, matter, time and space.

Souls may be bound to rebirth; perfected (*siddha*) by ethics and religious disciplines, and released from rebirth.

The material is whatever may have colour, smell, taste and touch. It is either atomic, or composite and macroscopic. Time is a basic reality and causes our experience of past, present and future. Space is single and limitless in extent.

Souls essentially have the properties of omniscience, will and feelings. The soul is an entity that both continues through time and is also continually changing. Bondage to rebirth involves the contraction of the soul's proper features and involves the misidentification of the soul with the body.

Moral conduct (especially non-violence – *ahimsa*), austere self-denial (*tapas*), withdrawal of the senses from the environment, and meditation are the means to release from rebirth (*moksha*). They prevent the influx of fresh *karma* and destroy *karmic* residues. Release is the manifestation of the soul's true nature as omniscient and so on once defects such as passionate attachments (*raga*) have ceased.

Karma is a sort of material substance that adheres to the soul. Souls are conditioned by morally good and bad *karmic* influxes (*asrava*) that impede their innate powers and tie them to particular sequences of embodied experiences. *Karma* and embodiment can only be burnt off by religious practices.

There are eight forms of *karma*: four harmful and four not harmful. The worst sort is deluding *karma*, which causes attachment to false beliefs and the incapacity to lead a religiously virtuous life. It has to be eliminated first. Other harmful varieties prevent the efficient functioning of the intellect and senses, and suppression of the soul's natural omniscience. The positive sorts condition possible types of experience as pleasant or otherwise, how one is reborn, the length of one's life and one's status in a species.

See *anekanta-vada*

Further reading: Balcerowicz 2000; Dundas 1992; Ganeri 2001a; Halbfass 1992; Jaini 1979 and 2000

Jaina ethics: *Jaina* monks and nuns, who have no possessions beyond the most basic necessities, vow to abstain from harming living creatures (*ahimsa*), lying, theft, sexual malpractice and attachment to worldly objects. They eat only vegetarian food prepared specially for them and there is a stress on fasting. Soul and matter are closely associated, so any type of action has moral as well as physical effects.

The laity's vows include non-injury, truthfulness and honesty in commercial dealings and charity to the monastic order. They are committed to honest ways of acquiring wealth, to the avoidance of sexual impropriety and to the renunciation of attachment to possessions. In addition, they should cultivate proper states of mind, undertake pilgrimages to sacred sites, meditate, fast and confess their failings and request forgiveness. Householders, frequently members of the merchant class, observe the Hindu *caste* system. Intermarriage and food sharing with Hindus is acceptable.

Actions performed out of ignorance and under the sway of the passions of anger, pride, self-deception and greed attract karmic influxes into the souls and restrict their potentialities. The purpose of religious life is to purge the soul of *karma*.

In their quest for self-perfection and dissociation from gross and *karmic* forms of matter (*moksha*: liberation), monks undertake a rigorous discipline whose goal is the prevention of *karmic* infiltration by the control of mental, verbal and physical acts, by taking care not to harm living creatures. They exercise the virtues of patience, humility, straightforwardness, purity, honesty, restraint, austerity, renunciation, chastity and obedience to elders in the community. They reflect on the impermanence of phenomena, human helplessness, transmigration, individual solitude, the difference between soul and body, physical impurity, the actuality of *karmic* influxes, the means to blocking *karmic* influxes, individual responsibility for salvation, the rarity of enlightenment and the truth of the teaching of the saints. The elimination of already accumulated *karma* begins once the acquisition of fresh *karma* has been prevented by the discipline of self-control.

Further reading: Dundas 1992; Jaini 1979 and 2000

Jainism: a renunciatory religious movement whose goal is individual self-perfection. It is believed to have been founded by *Vardhamana Mahavira* in the latter half of the sixth century BCE in northwestern India. *Mahavira* (the *Jina* or 'Victor') is considered to be the successor to twenty-three previous omniscient teachers or 'ford-makers' (*tirthankara*) who enable souls to cross the river of transmigratory existence. Like early Buddhism it is a renunciatory reaction against the *Vedic* ritualism of the Brahmin priesthood. By 79 CE when the movement split into the *Digambaras* ('sky-clad', that is, naked) and the *Shvetambaras* ('white-clad'), its main doctrines were settled. *Umasvati*'s *Tattvarthasutra* (fourth century CE) is a compendium of *Jaina* metaphysics. Other important works are the sixth-century *Mallavadin*'s 'Twelve-spoked Wheel of Perspectives' (*Dvadashara-nayacakra*) and *Siddhasena*'s *Nyayavatara*.

Further reading: Dundas 1992; Jaini 1979 and 2000

Jati: naturally occurring kind of entities that share the same generic property (*samanya*) or structural form (*akriti*).

See **caste**

Further reading: G. Bhattacharya 1989; Halbfass 1992; Matilal 1986

Jati-badhaka: criteria devised by the *Nyaya-Vaisheshika* philosopher *Udayana* to distinguish the objectively real universal properties (*samanya*) present by inherence in metaphysical and natural kinds from other general properties (*upadhi*).

1. A universal must group many instances. This rules out 'skyness', 'temporality' and 'spatiality' as well as *Devadattaness*, which belongs to the unique individual man called *Devadatta*.
2. Synonyms such as potness and jarness and the various words for cognition are terms referring to the same types of entity. Universals are not generated by

language. 'Beastness', although applicable to horses, cows and tigers since it is shorthand for a family of features, is not a genuine universal. A true universal is unanalysable.

3. No object possesses two universals, unless one is hierarchically nested in the other. Kinds cannot overlap or be intermingled in the same substrate. We might call the same creatures insects and parasites but this would not be a classification into different kinds. If two properties are present in an individual and one is not naturally included in the other, they cannot both be universals.

4. A universal cannot be the substrate of another universal, on pain of infinite regress.

5. A universal cannot conflict with the nature of its substrate. Ultimate differentia (*vishesha*), being unique, by definition lack a common property.

6. A universal must be capable of being related to its substrates. No universal can be inherent in inherence.

Further reading: G. Bhattacharya 1989; Ganeri 2001a; Potter 1977

Jiva-atman: the soul in its embodied condition, subject to *karma*, space and time.

Jivan-mukti: the view held by some **Advaita-Vedantins** that one can have achieved salvation (*mukti*) while still living in the world. The person who has realised that it is fundamentally mistaken to think of reality in terms of any differences whatsoever, who no longer understands himself as an individual subject of thought, feeling and agency, and who has accordingly renounced the world of everyday social interactions, may be considered to have realised the identity of the Inner Self with the Absolute

Reality (*Brahman*). At the falling away of the body, he will be liberated (*mukta*) from the series of births. Meanwhile, he awaits the natural exhaustion of his remaining stock of *karma*, at which point he will be released from rebirth.

Jnana (cognition): according to *Nyaya-Vaisheshika*, a cognition is a type of quality (*guna*) that occurs the principle of identity or soul (*atman*). Cognitions are understood as one-off psychological episodes, concrete unique occurrences (rather than as beliefs, which are settled dispositions, or what are understood as propositions in the Western tradition), receptive of information about the environment that causes them. Cognitions may be true or false. Some are stored as memories and may feature in complex thoughts.

While playing a crucial role in the subject's interaction with the physical world, cognitions are not aware of themselves, in accordance with the principle that nothing can exercise its proper function on itself. We are primarily aware of the world outside the mind, not our own thoughts. A cognition is a particular thought that always has some object, real or imagined: it is always awareness *of* something.

A cognition is consciously registered when it becomes the object of another thought (*anuvyavasaya*). The subject does not have to be explicitly aware that they know something to have a piece of knowledge. All that is required is that the cognitive state be the result of a reliable causal process.

There are two varieties of cognitive episodes: preconceptual (*nirvikalpa*), and conceptual and expressible in words (*savikalpa*). The former may be compared to glancing at a scene without noticing anything in particular (indeed it may not even be explicitly registered in consciousness). But an explicitly manifest conceptual cognition has a complex content (*vishayata*) that registers information about the matter and structure of its objects. The cognition verbalised as 'this is a pot' has the content: there is an individual pot qualified by potness, that is the locus of the quality-particular blue, which is qualified by blueness. A key point here is that the intellect is not creative: the mind has not added anything. It has just analysed and identified information about objects with properties in the external world. No veil of ideas falls between perception and its objects.

Further reading: Matilal 1986; Mohanty 1992

Jnana-karma-samuccaya-vada: the view that release from the series of births is attainable by a combination of right actions, both moral and ritual, and understanding. Insight into the truth about God and the soul is put into practice in the dutiful performance of one's prescribed social and religious duties in an unselfish, disinterested spirit. Such enlightened activity will not generate *karma* that personalises and binds one to rebirth. This is a religious path that reconciles the institutions of renunciation (*samnyasa*) and the performance of the rituals prescribed in the orthodox *Vedic* scriptures.

Jnana-marga (intuitive insight as the path to salvation): the view that release (*moksha*) from the series of births under the sway of *karma* is achievable through intuitive understanding of the true nature of reality and of the soul. This sort of insight, typically into the identity of the soul (*atman*) and the Supreme Being (*Brahman*), is the culmination of a long spiritual discipline involving the ascetic renunciation (*samnyasa*) of everyday activity, reflection upon the scriptures, and profound meditative contemplation.

Jnatata (the property of having been known): in opposition to Buddhists such as *Dharmakirti*, who maintained that we cannot distinguish objects from our awareness of objects (*sahopalambha-niyama*), the *Purva Mimamsaka* realist philosopher *Kumarila Bhatta* insists that no experiences are just generated by consciousness. Consciousness has no perspective upon itself and is not self-aware, as one thing cannot possess two operations simultaneously. It only has the power to manifest or reveal objects and is not reflexive or self-revealing (*sva-prakasha*) because a cognition, while illuminating an object cannot also illumine itself. He argues that just as we have no direct perception of the sensory faculties but infer their existence from the fact that we have experiences of colours and so on, so the existence of consciousness is inferred from the fact that external objects are known. There is no experience of cognition unless some object is known. He holds that knowledge is a type of action (*kriya*), not formed entity. As a realist, he insists on a difference between objects (*artha* – things) and objects-as-known (*vishaya* – mental content). Only actions can make a difference and bring about a difference in what is acted upon. The act of knowing changes the object into something known. We are not aware of the act of knowing at the time when it occurs. That it has happened is inferred from the fact that the property knowness (*jnatata*) is found to have been produced in some object. We know that we know something by a type of inference (*arthapatti*) from this effect in the object, not by looking within.

The soul, the bearer of the good and bad consequences of one's – especially ritual – actions does not reveal itself as the subject in acts of knowing. Rather, it is the object of the thought 'I', which does not in itself luminously manifest one's basic identity. Its existence is inferred as that which must be the continuing subject of experience.

That the thought 'I' contains no reference to spatial or temporal limitation means that the soul is an eternal and omnipresent spiritual essence. It is linked to the here and now by *karma* and embodiment.

Further reading: Kajiyama 1998; Matilal 1986; Mohanty 1992

Kalpana (conceptual construction): the activity of minds projecting what they take to be objective reality. Buddhist philosophers emphasise the activity of the mind in imposing structures on amorphous reality. This is opposed to the *Nyaya-Vaisheshika* realist view that the mind is confronted by an independent, ready-made physical world of persisting objects governed by natural laws. The latter view is that continuous individual identities, natural kinds, generic properties, qualities and some types of relation are objective realities that are discovered by the mind and articulated in our conceptual scheme. The Buddhists say that those categories are mental constructions. While the objective realm consisting of a flux of evanescent unique particulars (*svalakshana*) may have implicit configurations, the precise nature of its organisation (if any there is) eludes us. In fact, we are parts of the same process and not really independent observers. Nevertheless we can and do create conceptual schemes that help us to find our way.

See *padartha*, *vikalpa*
Further reading: Matilal 1986

Karaka: in Sanskrit grammar, factors participating in an action or event. They capture the deep structure of a proposition that can be expressed in different sentences. 'The man cuts the wood with an axe' and 'The wood is cut by the man with an axe' have the same *karaka*-structure. The *karakas* are:

Karta: the agent. This is independent relative to the other aspects of the action.

Karman: what the agent most desires is called 'object'.

Apadanam: that which is the fixed point of departure is called 'starting point'.

Sampradanam: that which one aims at as the object of one's action is called 'recipient'.

Karanam: that which is most effective is called 'instrument'.

Adhikaranam: substratum is called 'locus'.

There is a verse, 'The master of the factors in relation to action and inaction, whether it is currently active or not, is the factor called the agent.' Which means that conscious selves, enduring through time, are responsible for their moral and ritual actions. In events involving human actions, the selves are what hold together a sequence of fleeting events as a causal process and underpin continuities. The stable and enduring *atman*, which is given in experience but not produced by it, is undetermined by space and time.

See *Karana-vada*

Karana (cause according to *Nyaya-Vaisheshika*): cause is what *invariably* occurs *before* the effect. It is an indispensable prior condition. Cause and effect are distinct entities. The effect is called the counter-positive (*pratiyogin*) of its own prior absence. It originates as a novel product. It did not pre-exist in a potential state.

Nyaya-Vaisheshika recognises three types of causes. A piece of cloth is a whole product. Its underlying cause (*samavayi-karana*) is the threads (its parts) from which it is woven. The underlying cause is always a type of substance (*dravya*). The whole product exists in its parts by the relation of inherence (*samavaya*). In addition, the finished product is the underlying cause of its colour. Qualities (*guna*) need substances: they do not exist in their own right. So a substance is the underlying cause (indispensable condition) of the qualities inhering in it.

The companion cause (*asamavayi-karana*) is the combination of the threads by the relation of conjunction, which is a type of *guna*. It needs to belong to a substance. That substance is the threads. Also, the colours of the threads are the companion cause in respect of the produced colour of the finished product. The companion cause is always a quality (or motion).

The efficient causes (*nimitta-karana*) are the weaver's activity and apparatus.

See *Asatkaryavada*

Karana-vada: the Buddhists' belief in the essentially temporal nature of all entities involves a repudiation of the theory upheld by mainstream Brahminical orthodoxy that events and actions can be analysed in terms of specific real factors (*karaka*) such as a fixed starting point, the autonomous agent, objects and instruments. According to the Buddhists, there are just processes or sequences of events (*karana-vada*). Events follow other events but there are no real causal connections between them. It is a natural fact that some things happen in regular sequence but differentiation into agent, action, object, result and instrument is just a matter of human convenience reflected in the grammatical structures of language. It follows that individual people are just aspects of an event, enjoying no special significance.

Karma: the belief shared by Hindu, Buddhist and Jaina traditions that deliberately performed actions generate a
residue that stays with the agent until future circumstances are appropriate for its fruition in their experience.
Everyone has an inherited store of merit and demerit and
it is this that makes them the person and character that
they are. Hindus and Jains think that *karma* is associated
with the soul (*atman*), which is the constant principle
that remains the same through the succession of embodied lives. Buddhists reject the soul and think that *karma*
is a natural mechanism organised into streams of experiences. They also insist that it is the intention with which
the action is done that is morally significant.

There are three types: *karmic* dispositions whose consequences are manifested in the present life; *karmic* dispositions latent in the present life that will be actualised
in future lives; fresh *karma* that is the product of actions
being performed in this life.

The theory is not deterministic in that one's character
and life have been imposed from the outside. *Karma* is a
matter of what one chooses and does oneself.

Further reading: Gombrich 1994; Halbfass 1991;
O'Flaherty 1980

Karman (action/motion): according to *Vaisheshika*, this is
one of the objectively real types of features (*padartha*)
belonging to the cosmos. Motions (elevation and descent,
expansion, contraction and change of place) are transitory properties of persisting entities. It is also the efficient cause of conjunction or the putting together of two
objects.

Karma-nirapeksha (regardless of *karma*): the view that when
at the end of a period of cosmic retraction (*Pralaya*)
God produces a new universe, his organisation of the
initial state of affairs is totally independent of the

accumulated merit and demerit of conscious beings. The worry that while the divine freedom is unconstrained, God appears indifferent to human morality prompts the contrary view that he takes account of the moral status of beings (*Karma-sapeksha* – having regard to *karma*).

Ramanuja cuts the Gordian knot by effectively assimilating the concept of *karma* to that of the will of God. What we call good actions and their beneficial consequences are actions pleasing to God which he rewards accordingly.

Kevala-anvayi see *Hetu*

Kevala-vyatireka see *Hetu*

Kshanikatva (momentariness): Buddhist doctrine that whatever exists in dependence upon causes and conditions is momentary. An instant lasts just long enough for it to be replaced by another similar one. The essential temporality of being means that what appear to be enduring entities with a stable nature are at base level successions of phases. If nothing persists as the same through time, we live in a world in which basically impersonal states of affairs are constantly being replaced by others. Many Buddhists equated existence with the capacity for being causally effective or actually functioning (*arthakriya-karitva*).

The argument for universal momentariness is that destruction is a type of non-being or absence (*abhava*). Absences cannot be brought about or made. So destruction does not depend upon a cause outside itself. If anything is destructible, it must self-destruct. This means that its nature is to self-destruct. So this must happen immediately upon its occurrence. Every element of existence is naturally subject to destruction. So every element of existence is destroyed as soon as it comes into existence.

If this is true, there can be no real change. The Buddhists deny that something with a stable identity can change if change means becoming something else while staying the same thing but with different properties. There is no intrinsic change: only successive replacement.

The destruction of things is spontaneous because this is the nature of things. If something perishes by nature, it perishes on coming into existence. If something perishes on coming into existence, it is momentary. Thus there is no movement or change. There is only the arising of the next moment in many physical and mental series.

Further reading: Mookerjee 1975

Kumarila Bhatta (625–75 CE): a follower of the *Purva Mimamsaka* tradition, Kumarila was a realist philosopher whose major works include the *Shlokavarttika* and *Tantravarttika* commentaries on *Shabara*'s commentary on the *Mimamsa Sutras* of *Jaimini*.

A resolute opponent of Buddhism, *Kumarila* thinks that the individual soul (*atman*), really beyond space and time, is the centre of agency (*karta*) and experience (*bhokta*). Cognitions are formless (*nirakara*) acts. In each cognition, the non-creative mind is originally a blank slate (not a stock of concepts, memories and expectations conditioning the mode in which information is registered and interpreted) receiving information via the senses, about a world of objects. No possibly distorting inner realm of preconceptions intervenes between awareness and external objects. Cognitions are intrinsically truthful (*svatah pramanya*). That is to say, cognitions are assumed to be reliable. Even errors and dreams refer to realities experienced elsewhere. He thinks that there are two varieties of perception: a pre-linguistic and pre-conceptual (*nirvikalpa*) undifferentiated observation, comparable to the awareness of babies and the mute, of the object as an undifferentiated whole; this may be followed by a conceptual awareness involving an explicit grasp of the object in its individuality with its real properties including its generic form (*akriti*).

The absolute validity of the beginningless, authorless (*apaurusheya*) and infallible *Vedic* scriptures commanding ritual performances follows from the simple fact that they are perceived. They are our only means of knowing about that which lies outside experience, revealing something that would otherwise be unknown.

The relation between a *Vedic* word and its referent is direct, innate and constant. Such words primarily stand for everlasting generic properties (*samanya*) expressed in natural kinds (*jati*) and generic structures (*akriti*) of individuals. This is why and how they may also apply to individual entities (*vyakti*).

Kumarila accepts that language may express facts (*siddha*) as well as things to be done (*sadhya*). But the only type of language that is a source of knowledge in its own right is that of the *Vedic* ritual instructions (*vidhi*) because what is factual is already established by perception and inference. In accordance with the maxim, 'Not even the stupid act without some end in view', *Kumarila* thinks that the *Vedic* imperatives (*vidhi*) only motivate people who have an interest in the promised results of prescribed actions.

See ***anupalabdhi-pramana***, ***jnatata***, ***Prabhakara Mishra***

Further reading: Halbfass 1991; Hiriyanna 1993; Jha 1964

Lakshana-artha (non-literal word-meaning): Indian philosophers of language thought that words may have different
sorts of significances, according to the context of use. The
literal sense (*abhidha*, *mukhya-artha*) is innate in a word
and is usually directly understood. But sometimes it is apparent that the literal meaning of a word is impossible in
the context and we have to assume a non-literal meaning.
We cannot substitute any meaning. We have to be able to
justify the adoption of a non-literal meaning. There must
be some relationship between the primary and secondary
significances. For instance: 'Give food to the staff-holders'
means 'Give food to the Brahmins' because Brahmins always carry staffs. In 'The village on the Ganges', the word
'Ganges' must be taken in the secondary sense of 'bank
of the Ganges' because villages do not float. 'The umbrellas are coming' means that people with umbrellas are
coming.

Later writers say that there are three types of non-literal
word-meanings:

1. *Jahallakshana* (total secondary predication). 'There is
   a village on the Ganges', where the primary sense of
   'Ganges' disappears and is replaced by 'bank of the
   Ganges'.
2. *Ajahallakshana* (retention of the primary sense plus
   adoption of a secondary sense). For example, 'The
   spears are coming', where 'spear' refers to both spears
   and their carriers.
3. *Jahadajahallakshana* (partial secondary predication):
   'The man is a lion'. Such properties as ferocity and so
   on that he shares with the lion are attributed to the

man, while those characteristics of lions that he lacks are eliminated from the sense of 'lion'. This is particularly important for *Advaita Vedantins*. They think that in the scriptural statement, 'That thou art', 'thou' stands for the individual self and 'that' for the Absolute Reality. But if the statement asserts the identity of the soul and the absolute, 'thou' must drop its normal meaning of human personality and just mean the self-evident and self-luminous soul.

Further reading: Bartley 2002; Gerow 2001; Ingalls, Masson and Patwhardan 1990

Lakshanam (definition) (generally – distinguishing mark): a definition distinguishes its object from whatever differs in nature from that object. It must cite at least one uniquely identifying characteristic (*asadharana-dharma*). For example, possession of the dewlap is cited in the case of the species cow, that being sufficient to distinguish cows from buffaloes with which they might be confused.

There is a distinction between essential and incidental definitions, the latter specifying a property that while not being essential to the object is one by which it can be known. The Supreme Being may be defined essentially as 'reality, knowledge, infinite', and incidentally as the cause of the cosmos where being the cause of the cosmos is not a necessary property of *Brahman*.

Because statements of definition have a primarily negative import, differentiating their subject from everything else, some thinkers in the *Advaita-Vedanta* tradition interpreted some *Upanishadic* statements as definitions of *Brahman*.

A definition must avoid the defects of: over-extension (*ativyapti*), for example, 'cows have horns'; under-extension (*avyapti*), where the definition fails to apply to some individuals, for example, 'cows are brown'; and inapplicability or impossibility (*asambhava*), where the definition misses the point altogether.

Further reading: Bartley 2002; G. Bhattacharya 1989; Ganeri 1999; Ingalls 1951

Lila (delight or sport): this is **Ramanuja**'s way of expressing the spirit in which God creates the world. It means totally free activity, entirely self-sufficient and without any extrinsic purpose. Creation is not something that God has to do in order to achieve something that he wants, for he lacks nothing.

Further reading: Lipner 1986

Lokayata see *Carvaka*

Madhva (1238–1317): *Vedantic* theologian who wrote commentaries on several *Upanishads*, the *Bhagavad Gita*, the *Brahma-Sutras* and the *Bhagavata Purana*. He insisted on the absolute supremacy of the god *Vishnu*, of whom he thought of himself as an incarnation. He thinks that there are differences in kind between the self-determined (*svatantra*), that is, *Vishnu* and the necessarily dependent (*paratantra*), that is, everything else. Differences obtain between God and the individual soul, between the infinite number of souls, between God and matter, between souls and matter and between the material entities. The world is real because it is known and protected by *Vishnu*. The gulf between the absolute and the finite is spanned by the divine will sustaining and supporting created being. Clearly, Madhva's *Vedanta* is not only opposed to non-dualism

(*Advaita-Vedanta*), but also distanced from other theistic forms of **Vedanta** such as **Ramanuja**'s *Vishishta-advaita* that posits links between God and the world of conscious and non-conscious entities.

Each individual entity possesses a uniquely individuating feature (*vishesha*). According to **Ramanuja**, all released souls have the same qualities. This raises a problem, the problem of differentiation. *Madhva* avoids this difficulty by positing a distinguishing factor other than *karma*.

There are three categories of souls: those who are liberated; possible candidates for liberation; those who are beyond salvation. Liberation consists in the realisation of a state of innate consciousness and bliss focused on the divinity and is unattainable without a combination of devotion (*bhakti*) and divine favour (*prasada*).

Exceptionally for a *Vedantin* but consistently with his dualistic emphasis, while accepting that God is the efficient cause of the universe, *Madhva* denies that he is also its material or substrative cause. The material cause (*prakriti*) is an eternal reality that is distinct from God while dependent upon God. He excites its transformation into the cosmos.

Further reading: Mesquita 2000; Sarma 2003; Sharma 1986

Madhyamaka Buddhism: the 'middle way' school of *Mahayana* Buddhism founded by **Nagarjuna** (c. 150 CE). The school divided into *Prasangikas*, who thought that the philosopher should not put forward any positive arguments but rest content with destroying those of the opponent, and the *Svatantrikas*, who accepted that arguments should be advanced in favour of the tenet that nothing whatsoever has a permanent identity or essence. Prominent thinkers of the former school include: *Buddhapalita*

(470–540 CE), *Candrakirti* (600–50 CE) who wrote the
Prasannapada and the *Madhyamakavatara*, and *Shan-
tideva* (685–763 CE), author of the *Bodhicaryavatara*.
Bhavaviveka (500–70 CE) is the most notable *Svatantrika*.
He wrote the *Prajnapradipa* commentary on **Nagarjuna**'s
Mulamadhyamika-karikas.

Further reading: Crosby and Skilton 1996; Murti 1955;
Ruegg 1981; Williams 1989 and 1998

Mala (original stain): according to most types of *Shiva*-
worship, a defect which suppresses the soul's innate capacities for universal knowledge and agency and which
is responsible for their subjection to the acquisition of
the merit and demerit (good and bad **karma**) that brings
about bondage to a series of births.

According to **Shaiva-Siddhanta**, it is a kind of substance (**dravya**) so can be only removed by action. Knowledge of its presence is not enough. *Mala* is likened to an
ocular cataract, mere awareness of whose presence does
not impair its effects and whose removal requires the action of the surgeon's instrument. The only actions that can
remove it are the initiation rituals and their sequels taught
by *Shiva* in the *Tantric* scriptures. *Mala* is thought of as
'ripening': at a critical point in this process, the aspirant
will be moved by *Shiva*'s grace (*anugraha*) to approach
the guru for initiation (*diksha*) into the cult.

Shiva creates the universe as a compassionate act for
the sake of bound souls who need spheres of experience
in which they may be freed from *mala* and **karma**.

Mala provides an answer to the question of why human beings have **karma** and are bound to rebirth.

For those *Shiva* worshippers who believe that he is the
sole reality and that all apparent differences are included
in his being, basic *mala* is the limited state of awareness
that is normal personality. The term is also applied to

the appearance of reality as diversified into subjects and objects (*mayiya-mala*). *Karma-mala* is the belief that the true self is really conditioned by the moral quality of one's actions.

Further reading: Goodall 1998

Manas (mind or inner sense): according to *Nyaya-Vaisheshika*, the soul or self (*atman*) is a non-conscious principle of continuity. It becomes conscious whenever it is associated with thoughts, feelings and acts of will belonging to a particular embodied life. It is a matter of natural fact that sensory receptors (*indriya*) transmit a range of information about the objective environment to a physical faculty called *manas* which operates as a central processor coordinating that information and selecting what is relevant. In conjunction with the principle of identity or soul, the *manas* is instrumental in the conversion of some stimuli into feelings, the translation of some items of cognitive input into conscious thoughts with practical applications (storing some as memories), and the transformation of some affective responses into acts of will. Thoughts, feelings and intentions thus become temporary properties attaching to the soul-principle and a subject of knowing, agency and experience is created. Intelligence, feelings, memories and volitions are generated in the psycho-somatic complex whose unity over time is guaranteed by the enduring presence of the principle of identity.

Further reading: Chakrabarti 1999

Mandana Mishra (650–700 CE): a theorist of *Purva Mimamsa* ritualism and non-dualist *Advaita Vedanta*, whose most important work is the *Brahmasiddhi*.

His vision is that there is a single reality (*Brahman*) underlying everything. It is just undifferentiated consciousness. So differences are not ultimate realities. Finite individuals are subject to a basically distorted worldview that conceals the reality by superimposing diversity upon it. A force called 'beginningless misconception' (*avidya*) is responsible for the appearance of differences between selves, cognitions and objects. *Avidya* is connected with sorrow, delusion and passion. It conceals one's true nature, creating the illusion that one is an individual agent, which is the root cause of rebirth.

The relationship between *Brahman* and *avidya* is indefinable as real or unreal (*anirvacaniya*). Were *avidya* the same as *Brahman*, release would be impossible. If it is a positive entity (*bhava-rupa-avidya*) independent of *Brahman*, non-dualism is contradicted. Were it absolutely non-existent, there would be neither bondage nor worldly transactions (*vyavahara*).

Scripture is the authoritative source of knowledge (*pramana*) about the absolute reality that is already implicit in every preconceptual awareness. Negative scriptural statements teach the unreality of phenomenal diversity and eradicate *avidya* while positive ones affirm the sole reality of *Brahman* with which the soul (*atman*) is identical.

While the *Advaita* theorist **Shankara** thinks that the *Vedic* ritual actions are dispensable in the quest for liberation, Mandana's view is that all *Vedically* enjoined action is purificatory and predisposes towards realisation of one's true identity. He holds that release from rebirth requires a combination of knowledge and ritual action (*jnana-karma-samuccaya-vada*), a way especially suited to householders in normal society. Renunciation of all ritual actions (*samnyasa*) is a possible path to self-realisation but it is difficult. It is better that the knowledge gained from the scriptural texts teaching the identity of the soul and **Brahman** be intensified by the performance of ritual actions and contemplation.

Further reading: Halbfass 1995; Potter 1981; Thrasher 1993

Maya: this may mean the real material or substrative cause (*upadana-karana*) from which the universe of worlds emerges and into which it is reabsorbed (*pralaya*). Dualistic theologians think that it is a complex raw material that is stimulated by God to produce types of bodies, faculties and material realities, including space and time. By contrast, some non-dualists (see *Advaita*) say that *maya* is the Supreme Reality's power of projecting the world comprising matter, differences, limited personal individuality and change. But both the power and the projected cosmos are really not different from the essentially conscious nature of the Supreme. So matter and individuality are not ultimate facts but the way in which reality appears to us. Illusion operates whenever we understand reality as something independent of the foundational Absolute Reality.

Shankara sometimes compares anything illusory, in particular differences grounded in matter and individual agency, to *maya*, meaning a magical trick.

Further reading: Halbfass 1995

Moksha: final liberation from the series of embodied lives in the here and now (*samsara*). The ultimate goal of all paths to salvation, it is achievable by control over physical and mental processes (*yoga*), knowledge (*jnana-yoga*), selfless action, devotion to God (*bhakti-yoga*) or by a combination of some or all of them. Some theistic cults insist that it is given by God. It is *karma* that binds one to *samsara* and the achievement of liberation requires that one's stock of *karma* be completely exhausted.

For the *Mimamsaka* ritualists it is depersonalised individual consciousness beyond matter and time, attained by the meticulous performance of mandatory ritual actions, without attachment to their results.

Advaita Vedanta holds that it is the realisation of the identity of the inactive conscious soul with the Supreme Being (*Brahman*) that is static, pure consciousness and bliss. Theistic *Vishishta-advaita Vedanta* understands it as the soul's loving service to God in heaven. For *Samkhya-Yoga*, it is the isolation of individual and inactive centres of pure consciousness, the end of thought and feeling, in a dimension beyond time and matter. *Shaiva Siddhanta* says that it full manifestation of the soul's innate powers of knowledge and agency in supernatural spheres of existence. Other *Shiva*-worshippers understand it as the ecstatic recognition, typically through *yoga* and meditation, that one is not a self-contained individual but an aspect of the self-expression of the dynamic Universal Consciousness (*see Trika*).

For the Buddhist view, see: *Nirvana*.

Further reading: Lipner 1986; Ram-Prasad 2001

Momentariness see *Kshanikatva*

Mulamadhyamaka-karikas: this work by *Nagarjuna* is the foundational text articulating *Madhyamaka Buddhism*. Basic to *Nagarjuna*'s viewpoint are the claims that there are no unchanging, essential natures and that we cannot escape from the conceptual schemes that we take to describe reality. The categories and concepts with which we think are only mental fabrications and not really about anything. In the *Mulamadhyamaka-karikas*, *Nagarjuna* examines our ways of thinking and tries to show that they involve contradictions and thus cannot be true. What reality is in itself, we simply cannot know.

Crucial is the rejection of real causal relations and causal powers inherent in entities. It is impossible that

entities be self-created. But if we say that they are created from other things, this raises the question of what
produced those producers. The rejection of real causation
rules out the possibility of a final explanation.

He argues that there are no absolutes, no permanent
selves, so stable entities, no intelligible distinction between agents and actions, no relations apart from things
related, no intelligible distinction between past, present
and future times, and no sense can be made of the idea of
space.

Further reading: Garfield 1995; Murti 1955; Williams
1989

Nagarjuna (c. 150 CE): founder of *Madhyamaka* Buddhist
philosophy whose most important works are the
Mulamadhyamaka-karikas and *Vigrahavyavartani*. In
their attempt to frame an objective and complete description of reality, Buddhist *Abhidharma* philosophers
claimed that unobserved atomic factors (*dharmas*) are the
ultimately real entities. They compiled vast catalogues of
mental and material atoms, which are the building blocks
of all kinds of subjects, experiences and objects. They
thought that the *dharmas* possessed intrinsic natures or
essences (*svabhava*) and that this distinguished them from
the macroscopic compound entities that they make up.
Nothing made of parts is ultimately real. Essence here
means a nature that is unchanging, without beginning or
end, self-sufficient and independent of anything else. Nagarjuna insists that the *Abhidharma* outlook is contrary
to authentic Buddhist teaching which says that there are
no unchanging essences: everything is empty (*shunya*) of

inherent nature (*svabhava*). He says that entities with essential natures would have to be uncaused or self-created, which is impossible. There cannot be any *dharmas* with essences or immutable natures. If reality basically consisted of *dharmas* possessing essence, the universe would be static and there would be no changes. If the unsatisfactory round of existences (*samsara*) had essence, there would be no possibility of *nirvana* and if *nirvana* had essence, there would be no *samsara*. Buddhists believe that everything in the world arises in dependence upon causes (*hetu*) and conditioning factors (*pratyaya*). All Buddhists accept that conditioned entities lack essence. *Nagarjuna* insists that whatever is interdependently originated (*pratitya-samutpada*) is also devoid of essential nature. Lack of essence does not follow simply from the fact of being interdependently originated. There cannot be any essences.

If there are no essences, there are no stable entities with clearly demarcated boundaries or identities. But *Nagarjuna* is not a nihilist. The absence of essences does not mean that we do not inhabit a world of changing realities.

He denies that causation is a real relation. Events happen in succession and our minds impose associations that we treat as causal realities. But we do not see causal forces. Moreover, there are no types, kinds or classes of entities with intrinsic causal powers.

If there are no essences, the *Abhidharma* distinction between conventional reality and ultimate reality (*dharmas* with essential natures) collapses. There is no difference between *samsara* and *nirvana*. We cannot produce a complete and correct description of reality that is independent of any particular perspective. It is pointless to entertain the possibility that there is an ultimate truth accessible to the finite conceptual capacities and schemes,

which are relative to human interests. There are only particular points of view. No content can be given to the
expression, 'absolute conception of reality'. The truth is
just that there is no ultimate description of reality. This is
what he calls 'the emptiness of emptiness'.

The realisation that everything is empty puts an end
to conceptual construction. That is to say, we cease to
believe that our concepts are describing objective reality.
Insight into emptiness, the realisation that there are no
absolute truths to be found, leads to a compassionate outlook and mental peace, as one is no longer disappointed
by the search for certainties.

In the *Vigrahavyavartani* he defends an extreme form
of scepticism: you cannot determine what the reliable
means of knowledge (*pramana*) are unless you have de-
cided what things there are to be known (*prameya*); you
cannot ascertain what things there are to be known, until
you have identified the means of knowing.

When *Nagarjuna* says that he is not proposing a thesis
of his own, he means that he is not presenting an al-
ternative version of the *Abhidharmika* realists' comprehensive descriptions of objective reality. Moreover, attachment to dogmatically held viewpoints is spiritually
damaging.

See **Madhyamaka Buddhism, Shunyata**

Further reading: K. Bhattacharya 1998; Burton 1999;
Garfield 1995; Lindtner 1982; Murti 1955; Siderits 2003;
Williams 1989

Nairatyma (no soul): according to all Buddhist schools there
is no further fact called soul over and above the stream
of ever-changing experiences. We can claim this because
we have no cognition (*anupalabdhi*) of such an entity
although it is the sort of thing that would be known if it
existed.

Navya-Nyaya (New Nyaya): in response to critiques, especially those initiated by the *Advaita-Vedantin Shri Harsha*, of the coherence of their description of reality in categories (*padartha*) and of their theories about the reliable means of knowledge (*pramana*), logicians in the realist *Nyaya-Vaisheshika* tradition redefined their concepts and categories. They developed a rigorously defined technical philosophical language of some complexity. Their novelty consists in method rather doctrines, although *Raghunatha* suggests some radical economies about what may be considered to exist. Their opponents are *Advaita Vedantins* and *Purva-Mimamsakas* rather than Buddhists, the latter having virtually disappeared from India by the thirteenth century. Major thinkers include *Gangesha* (thirteenth century), author of the *Tattvacintamani*, *Raghunatha* (1475–1550), who wrote the *Didhiti* commentary on *Gangesha* and the *Padartha-tattva-nirupana*, a revolutionary work radically revising the received system of categories, and *Gadadhara* (seventeenth century), whose *Shakti-vada* ('Theory of Semantic Power') is a remarkable contribution to the philosophy of language.

Their argumentative techniques were put to good use by logicians belonging to the realist and dualist *Dvaita Vedanta* tradition.

Further reading: Ganeri 1999; Ingalls 1951; Matilal 1968; Mohanty 1966; Phillips 1996; Potter and Bhattacharya 1993

Neti Neti ('It is not thus'): the *Upanishads* provide the subject matter of theological reflection in the *Vedantic* schools. Some *Upanishadic* statements ascribe positive features to the Supreme Being while others characterise it in negative terms ('inactive', 'without qualities' 'changeless'). There is also the denial that the Supreme Being can be expressed in language and concepts. One such case is the designation of 'the reality of reality' as 'not thus, not thus' at *Brihadaranyaka Upanishad* 2.3.6. The *Advaita-Vedantin* thinker **Shankara** says that this helps us understand the nature of the ultimate reality by excluding from it every finite and variable factor. It expresses something that has no distinguishing features: neither name, form, action, difference, genus nor quality that are the grounds for the applications of words. Since the Absolute has no features, it cannot be described as 'this' or 'that'. The Absolute may be provisionally thought of in terms of name, form and action superimposed upon it. But we can only indicate what it is in itself by denying of it all descriptions that apply to aspects of the cosmos.

Brahman, the universal source beyond all oppositions, is not existent in the same way in which worldly objects are. We cannot say that *Brahman* and empirical objects exist in the same sense of 'exist'.

Shankara thinks that the descriptive *Upanishadic* statements do not convey saving knowledge directly but they help to turn the mind away from the world and towards what is divine. Even the most elevated thoughts do not express the ultimate truth since they belong to the sphere of *avidya* and presuppose the reality of differences.

Further reading: Bartley 2002

Nirakaravada (awareness is formless): the *Vaibhashika* Buddhists, *Nyaya-Vaisheshikas*, *Purva Mimamsakas* and *Vedantins* agree that consciousness scans and illuminates external objects without undergoing any intrinsic change. To say that awareness lacks form means that cognitions are differentiated by the objects that cause them. It does not commit one to the view that there is any undifferentiated consciousness or blank cognitions waiting for objects. The *Nyaya* school holds that, in a true cognition, the mental image is a copy of the object.

Fundamentally, this is the rejection of the views that what we experience is not physical objects but ideas in our minds, and that our perceptions of reality are just subjective interpretations.

See *sakara-vada*

Further reading: Kajiyama 1998; Matilal 1986; Mohanty 1992

Nirguna (featureless Absolute Being): *Advaita-Vedanta* tenet that the foundation of reality (*Brahman*) is an impersonal and indescribable conscious principle utterly devoid of any differentiating features or actions. The soul within everyone is identical with this formless reality. Intuitive realisation of this identity is the goal of purely mental spiritual discipline. Belief in the ultimate reality of any form of individuality and agency is mistaken.

Nirukta (*Nirvacana-shastra*): the meanings of many of the words in the ancient *Vedic* scriptures were obscure. The *Nirukta* tradition developed techniques for explaining these problematic words, which were widely deployed whenever some explanation of a term was called for. The view was that meanings were basically related to actions. Actions are signified by verbs. Nouns stand for aspects of events. The meaning of a noun derives from the meanings of verbs. The sounds of a word are the vehicles of its core meaning. The meaning of a problematic word may be understood from its grammatical formation and role in a context. But where this does not help, comparison between the sounds found in a word and the same sounds as found in verbs can reveal the meaning of a noun.

Examples: In *Abhidharma* Buddhism, the noun *dharma* stands for the basically real mental and material atomic factors. This is explained as *svalakshana* (its own unique feature) – *dharanad* (by supporting). *Dharanad* is derived from the verbal root *dhr* which has the general meaning 'continuing in existence' and 'support'.

Dravya means substance or a stable entity that continues more or less the same through time. This meaning derives from the verbal form *dravati* ('it runs') since a substance is a constant factor running through time.

Diksha means the initiation ritual into a cult. It is explained as that through which knowledge is provided (*di-yate*), and by which whatever contracts the soul's self-understanding is destroyed (*kshiyate*).

Atman (soul) is explained by the verb *apnoti*, meaning 'it pervades' and 'it obtains' since the soul pervades, controls and supports the body and cognitively grasps objects.

Further reading: Kahrs 1998

Nirvana: a basic Buddhist belief is that there is no substantial enduring Self or Soul (*atman*). *Nirvana* is liberation from the ultimately meaningless and unsatisfactory series of births after the extinction of the fires of craving, hatred and delusion. It is the end of individual personality and its selfish obsessions. The early traditions refer to the 'blowing out' of the fires of clinging, hostility and delusion, which means the end of suffering (*duhkha*). (The fires metaphor is deliberate. It refers to the three fires which the Hindu Brahminical householder was obliged to keep burning and which symbolised his life, responsibilities and attachments as a man in the world.) *Nirvana* is beyond being and becoming. It is unthinkable and indescribable. It is neither a heavenly state nor an oceanic consciousness into which individuals are absorbed. From our point of view, it is sheer nothingness.

According to the early Buddhist *Abhidharma* traditions *nirvana* may be attained while one is still alive through insight into the *Four Noble Truths* and by the suppression of the impure elements of existence, which have been rendered inoperative in relation to the skilled meditator. Meditation upon the transitory and composite (that is, not truly real) nature of everything experienced prevents the arising of future conditioned *dharmas* in a psycho-physical stream. *Parinirvana* or ultimate extinction occurs at death. The life in the world of the enlightened one (*arhat*) continues until the five constituents of personality (*Skandhas*: matter and form, feelings, perceptions, dispositions and conscious acts) are expended or 'burnt out'. After the death of the enlightened one, there is neither rebirth nor any form of experience.

The later south-east Asian *Mahayana* Buddhist traditions tend to understand *nirvana* more positively as an enlightened way of being in the world, total extinction being a remote horizon. The *Bodhisattva* (enlightened being), having realised the insubstantiality of all phenomena and the vanity of one's sense of self, is moved by compassion to bring to *nirvana* all suffering, transmigrating beings. A modern example is the Dalai Lama.

Further reading: Gombrich 1996; Williams 1989

Nirvikalpaka-pratyaksha (concept-free perception): after the Buddhist thinker *Dignaga*, who held that perceptual sensation and conceptual thought were completely different, *Nyaya* and *Purva Mimamsa* realist philosophers respond by distinguishing between two types of perception. The first is non-conceptual (*nirvikalpa*) awareness, arising from sensory impressions, of the object as an undifferentiated whole. This does not involve explicit recognition of the object's general and specific features. *Kumarila Bhatta* says that first there is observation, which is non-conceptual. It is produce by the pure object and is like the awareness of infants and mute people. The information received in pre-conceptual perception is translated into conceptual form in concept-laden perception (*savikalpa-pratyaksha*) that analyses the content of sensation and identifies the object in terms of the categories (*padartha*) of substance, generic property and particular-quality.

Ramanuja thinks that *nirvikalpaka-pratyaksha* is just as specific as *savikalpaka-pratyaksha*; the difference lies just in the fact that awareness of one individual does not involve cognition of the recurrence of a generic property in many individuals of the same kind.

Navya-Nyaya thinkers maintain that one is not directly aware of pre-conceptual awareness, which is knowable only by inference. *Savikalpa-pratyaksha* is the expression in concepts of the content of primary perception and always involves words. It comprehends the complex relationship between the object and its properties.

Further reading: Bartley 2002; Matilal 1986

Nirvishesha (absence of differentia): reflecting the experience of profound meditative contemplation in which the mind is emptied of distracting thoughts and feelings, *Advaita Vedanta* maintains that ultimate reality beyond all oppositions is changeless consciousness void of differentiating features.

Vedantins recognise sense-perception (*pratyaksha*), inference (*anumana*) and scriptural language (*shabda*) as reliable means of knowledge (*pramana*). Anything genuinely existent can in principle be known by one or more of those methods. Scripture is our only way of knowing anything outside the scope of sensory perception and inference. *Ramanuja* argues that the *Advaitin* cannot establish his view that reality is ultimately non-differentiated contentless consciousness. All *pramana*-based understanding is necessarily of particularised entities with identifiable features. If reality were non-differentiated, our recognised means of knowing could not operate.

Scriptural language cannot establish that reality is non-differentiated pure consciousness. The intrinsically composite and relational nature of the Sanskrit language reflects the complexity of that to which it refers.

Further reading: Bartley 2002

Nitya: usually translated as 'eternal' or 'permanent', this usually means 'without beginning and end' and is applied to whatever lacks prior and posterior forms of absence (*abhava*). It covers God, the souls, and the *Vedic* scriptures teaching social and religious duty (*dharma*) and liberation from continuous rebirth (*moksha*). *Anitya* means anything lasting for a time.

Nitya-dravya (eternal substances): according to the *Vaisheshika* description of the cosmos, these are atmosphere, time, space, souls (*atman*) and minds (*manas*) as well as the atoms comprising earth, water, light and air in addition. Being singular, no universal properties inhere in them. They are differentiated by their ultimate particularities (*vishesha*).

Noble Eightfold Path: Buddhist morality leading to the end of unsatisfactory existence through the elimination of craving, attachments, aversions and delusions. Unenlightened people believe in their own individuality, and are prey to sensual desires, malice, craving for more existences, self-glorification and self-obsession, and ignorance. The path consists of right views, right thoughts, right speech, right action, right livelihood, right effort, right mindfulness and right concentration. Right views and thoughts are classified as mind-purifying wisdom or insight into the fleeting and unsatisfactory nature of existence; right speech, action and livelihood are classified as moral conduct; right effort, mindfulness and concentration are classified as meditation (*samadhi*). Buddhists insist that virtue is necessary for the cultivation of meditation and insight. In early Buddhism, intention (*cetana*) is understood as determining the moral quality of an action. Morality consists in deliberate abstention from murder, theft, sexual misconduct, false speech, slander, harsh words, frivolous talk, covetousness, malice and false views. Right livelihood would preclude such occupations as arms-trading, dealing in drugs and alcohol, and butchering animals. *Samadhi* is the achievement of tranquillity through avoidance of distractions, and by suppression of sensory activity. Emphasis is placed upon mindfulness or exercising control over one's physical, mental and emotional states. *Samadhi* also involves the cultivation of goodwill, compassion, joy and equanimity.

The path is the 'middle way' between the self-indulgent and ascetic lives, neither of which lead to release from the desire-fuelled series of existences. What is needed is the elimination of the basic defects of craving, aversion and delusion. Buddhism claims to be a true universal morality. Its ethical principles are 'don't kill, don't steal, don't tell lies, avoid intoxicants and sexual misdemeanours'. It differs from *caste*-based Hinduism where what is morally right for a person depends upon their *caste* status.

Further reading: Conze 1959; Keown 1992; Siderits 2003

Number see *Samkhya*

Nyaya: one of the six orthodox Brahminical schools (*darshana*). Nyaya accepted the *Vaisheshika* categorisation (*padartha*) of reality and was chiefly concerned with questions of logic and how we can know anything. Major works and theorists include *Gautama Akshapada* (c. 150 CE), the author of the fundamental *Nyaya-Sutra*;

Vatsyayana (350–400 CE), author of the *Nyaya-Bhashya*; *Uddyotakara* (550–600 CE), author of the *Nyayavarttika*; *Vachaspati Mishra* (800–50 CE), author of the *Tatparyatika*; *Jayanta Bhatta* (850–900 CE), author of the *Nyayamanjari*; *Bhasarvajna* (900–50 CE), author of the *Nyayasara* and *Nyayabhushana*; and *Udayana*.

Nyaya theorists are direct realists about perception and hold that whatever exists is in principle knowable. All there really is is open to observation, either directly (*pratyaksha*) or indirectly (*anumana*, and testimony or *shabda*). The world is basically how it appears to commonsense. It causes our perceptions. Cognitions (*jnana*) are always and only the manifestation of mind-independent realities (including perceptible universals and relations) outside the mind. A cognitive episode may grasp the same physical object by the senses (*indriya*) of sight and touch when they are coordinated by the mind (*manas*). This concurrence proves both the integrated unity of the whole object (*avayavin*) and the identity of the continuous subject to which perceptions attach. The soul (*atman*) is an immaterial but essentially non-conscious principle of continuity. But it has the capacity to become temporarily the substrate of cognitive episodes, feelings and acts of will.

A cognition is not self-aware but requires a subsequent cognition (*anuvyavasaya*) to reveal it. This rejection of reflexivity is consistent with the insistence that we are primarily aware of a world outside the mind and not our ideas.

They hold that to be in a state of knowledge, it is not necessary that one actually knows that one knows. What is necessary is that one's true belief should have been arrived at by a reliable method.

The reliable means of knowledge (*pramana*) are: perception (*pratyaksha-pramana*), which is basic to our body-based interactions with the material world and is of two kinds: primary, non-verbal sensory awareness in which specific characteristics are not explicitly recognised for what they are (*nirvikalpaka-pratyaksha*) and awareness saturated by concepts and language (*savikalpaka-pratyaksha*) which identifies the given more specifically); inference (*anumana*) which is dependent upon information supplied by sensory perception; language (*shabda*), which is the testimony of experts.

They emphasise right understanding of the structures and operations of the cosmos as a path to release from rebirth. Given that the soul, although an individual principle of continuity, is not essentially conscious (although it becomes the substrate of cognitive episodes, feelings and acts of will) it is not something to be clung to. The state of release is one of non-consciousness. There is no pure happiness, because happiness is always pervaded by fear of its loss.

Further reading: G. Bhattacharya 1989; Ganeri 2001a; Ganeri 2001b; Matilal 1986, 1998 and 2002b; Potter 1977

P

Padartha (category of entities): according to *Vaisheshika*, these are the types of objectively real basic features that organise, structure and give identity to individual objects in the cosmos. (*Padartha* may also refer to a particular object belonging to a type of entities.) The categories are *dravya* (substantial continuants), *guna* (qualities or particular properties), *karma* (motions), *samanya* (generic properties), *samavaya* (inherence or internal relation), *vishesha* (individualising mark of atoms and souls) and *abhava* (absences). Types of features belonging to the seven categories are existent, knowable and nameable (if not by us, then by God).

If we say that Red Rum is a horse, we are categorising him as a substance (*dravya*). If we exclaim that he is a shining example of the family of horses, we are saying that he is an instance (*vyakti*) of the generic property horseness (*samanya* or *jati*). We can say that he is dark brown and of a given height and weight (*guna*), and that he can canter, gallop or walk (*karman*). Vets can also describe the natural integration (*samavaya*) of physical organs (parts) that makes him a whole persisting entity. As well as the individual object Red Rum, all those features are objective realities in their own right. They are not just ideas that we use to classify what we experience. The generic property horseness is a different kind of thing from the objects that it characterises. Colours and other qualities are objective realties. The property brown is different from objects that are brown. Running differs from individual entities that run.

Belief that integral to the structure of the cosmos are categorical distinctions between properties and the individual objects possessing them is one of the key points that distinguishes most Hindu (and *Jaina*) philosophers from their Buddhist opponents. The Buddhists deny that when we see a pot, we also detect a difference between a whole and its parts, or between the object and its particular qualities, or see the object as an individual instance of a separate universal. In fact, they think that temporary collections of features are what we (mistakenly) call objects, investing them with a permanence that is nowhere to be found.

Further reading: G. Bhattacharya 1989; Halbfass 1992; Potter 1977

Padmapada (700–50 CE): *Advaita-Vedantin* author of the *Pancapadika*. Whereas *Shankara* understands ignorance (*avidya*) as human misconception (*mithya-jnana*) and our innate tendency to confuse (*adhyasa*) the true self and what it is not, *Padmapada* maintained that it is the cause of misconception and superimposition. He described *avidya* as a material (*jada*) force that is the underlying cause of the world-appearance. *Avidya* veiled the intact nature of **Brahman** and in association with the workings of **karma** and memory traces of previous cognitions produced the illusion of limited selfhood that is the substrate of individual experience and agency. He thought that the limited self is a finite reflection (*pratibimba*) of **Brahman**.

Further reading: Halbfass 1995; Potter 1981

Paksha: the subject in an inference. It is the problematic case under consideration. When we wonder whether there is fire (*sadhya*) on the mountain, the mountain is the *paksha*. We notice that there is smoke (*hetu*) on the mountain and remember the generalisation, 'wherever there is smoke, there is fire'. This may be supported by similar and dissimilar instances: the kitchen (*sapaksha*) where smoke and fire invariably co-occur and the lake (*vipaksha*) that never harbours fire and never sees smoke, although the morning mist rising from it may sometimes have wrongly suggested otherwise.

Further reading: Ganeri 2001b

Paramartha-sat (ultimate reality/truth): reality as it is in itself, objective in the sense that it is independent of finite observers and their thoughts.

Basic to Buddhism is a distinction between objective reality (absolute truth) and conventional reality that is a matter of human experience (*vyavahara, samvriti, prajnapti*). It is undeniable that we have a sense of ourselves as embodied experiencers and agents with a history, a now, and future expectations. We may always feel that we are the same thing and, even when we are troubled about the variability of our identity, reflection suggests a persisting single subject that asks the questions. Moreover, we know that our previous actions and experiences don't just linger in the memory but often have a real impact on our present circumstances. And the way we live now affects our future. Buddhism does not deny that all this is real human experience. But it is just human convention. The absolute truth is that objective reality is an impersonal flux of instants. Some of the basic constituents of existence automatically form streams of experience that are interpreted as continuous selves The constituents behave in such a way that individuals impose cause–effect relations upon successive occurrences that we interpret as our decisions, actions and their consequences. But the truth is that reality is basically a field of mental and material particles. What is really happening is independent of human intellect and will, which are not fundamental to the process.

Advaita Vedanta makes a similar distinction between absolute and conventional reality. But according to them there is a single absolute reality beyond all oppositions, which is static, featureless consciousness. Upon it we superimpose the differentiated conventional world of individual centres of awareness and agency, and objects.

Parartha-anumana (inference for the sake of other people): this is a fully elaborated sequence of statements that follow one another logically. It is used for proving a point in public debate. By contrast, there is *svartha-anumana* (inference for oneself) which just involves one's thoughts and does not make public assertions. The form is simpler: 'There is smoke on the mountain and smoke is always accompanied by fire.'

See *Anumana*

Paratah Prakasha (non-reflexivity of consciousness): this is the view that a cognitive state is not known to the subject immediately upon its occurrence. The *Nyaya-Vaisheshikas* and *Bhatta Mimamsakas* (see **Kumarila**) deny that conscious states, which are exclusively defined in terms of the manifestation of objects external to the mind, are intrinsically reflexive or self-revealing (*svayam prakasha*). The *Nyaya* holds that a perceptual state may be revealed once it has occurred by another perceptual state (*anuvyavasaya*). The standard objections to this position are that it involves an infinite regress and that dependence upon an extraneous factor for illumination is a common characteristic of the inert. The ultra-realist followers of **Kumarila** say that cognitions, in themselves formless and receptive, are acts (*kriya*) which produce the temporary property of being known (*jnatata*) in the external object. We know that cognition has occurred by inference from this effect not by introspection.

Further reading: Matilal 1986

Paratah pramanya: *Nyaya* philosophers hold that a cognition is true when it corresponds to some reality external to the mind. They recognise that we cannot check the truth of a cognition by stepping outside ourselves and comparing our thoughts with objective reality. We need some other form of testing, such as successful activity following the cognition which reveals its truth. So they make a distinction between the origins of a belief and what makes it true. Truth stands in need of confirmation, it is not self-evident. We infer that a cognition was true on the basis of its having generated successful practice. So knowledge is not transparently true. The objection to this is that the confirmatory awareness stands in need of confirmation and so on. The *Nyaya* response is that the experience of success is sufficient to check the need for further corroboration.

From the very beginning (when the Buddha said, 'Don't take my word for it, see if it works'), Buddhists insisted that the truth of a claim is revealed in consequent success-ful activity. *Nagarjuna* argues that since a cognition can neither be validated by itself nor by another cognition, no sense can be made of the notion that there are definite means of knowledge.

See *Svatah pramanya*

Parinama (modification): this is when a persisting entity loses a characteristic and acquires another without there being any change in its essential nature. The subject (*dharmin*) of the change remains basically the same. The idea was formulated in the *Samkhya* system in an attempt to artic-ulate the persistence of objects, while avoiding the ex-treme *Nyaya* view that when an object loses of gains a property it becomes another thing (see *Avayavin*). In general terms, parinama is restricted to what is physical: nothing subject to this sort of change can be the soul.

In theistic **Vedanta**, *parinama* means the emergence of the real cosmos from God who is its underlying real cause and superintendent. It is contrasted with *vivarta* (only apparent change), which means that the world is just an appearance concealing the undifferentiated Absolute Reality.

Paryudasa-pratisheda (nominally-bound or term negation): the term signifying negation is connected with any word that is not a finite verb. For example, 'Bring a non-Brahmin' tells us to bring a person, but not a Brahmin. Here, negation has a positive implication.

See *Prasajya-pratishedha*

Pervader-pervaded relation: the pervader (*vyapaka*) occurs in all or more than the instances in which the pervaded (*vyapya*) occurs. Fire (*vyapaka*) pervades smoke (*vyapya*).

Of the two, it is the more inclusive feature. The presence of smoke implies the presence of fire. The situation is called 'pervasion' (*vyapti*). This state of affairs justifies the conclusion that wherever there is smoke there is fire. Oaks and elms are pervaded by the condition of being trees. Oaks and so on are pervaded by tree-ness. So we can reason that if something is an oak, then it is a tree. 'This is a tree (*sadhya*), because it is an oak (*hetu*).'

In negative terms, the absence or exclusion of the pervader entails the absence or exclusion of the pervaded. No fire, no smoke. No trees, no oak trees.

Prabhakara Mishra (625–75 CE): Hindu *Purva Mimamsa* theorist of ritual religion and author of the *Brihati* commentary on *Shabara*'s commentary on the *Mimamsa Sutras*. *Prabhakara*, like all *Mimamsas*, holds that the mind is the passive recipient of perceptual information about the environment. The perceiving mind does not see the world through an interpretative filter of ideas that might lead to distorted perceptions. If I mistake a piece of shell for silver, it may be because I am seeing fragments of silver in the shell. Alternatively, I am not distinguishing a representation of a present object with a memory of a real object. All cognitions must therefore be considered true in themselves. Error occurs when we confuse judgements. It must be borne in mind that his view is that reality is not something given: it has to be continuously created. The continuation of the cosmos depends upon the performance of ritual that brings about new reality.

Prabhakara and his school hold that in every cognitive act the soul is revealed as the subject simultaneously with the object by a self-luminous, reflexive awareness.

He holds that the *Vedic* ritual instructions (*niyoga*) have an automatic motivational force when heard by people whose ritual duty they command. They are thus like categorical imperatives that move to action regardless of what the agent desires.

Prabhakara restricts the authority (*pramanya*) of language to the ritual instructions found in the Vedic scriptures (*shastra*). Vedic injunctions (*niyoga*) relate to an interconnected reality that has to be brought about (*karya*). It follows that the smallest significant unit of language is the sentence. Already existent (*siddha*) objects do not need verbal testimony in order to be known and have their natures established because perception and inference are means of knowledge for them. Since the *Vedas* are primarily concerned with enjoining ritual action, they cannot be an authoritative source of knowledge (*pramana*) for the existence and description of a supposedly already existent entity such as the **Brahman** held to be the Supreme Being by the *Vedantic* schools. This is hotly contested by the various schools of **Vedanta**.

See *anvita-abhidhana*

Further reading: Buitenen 1956; Hiriyanna 1993; Jha 1911 and 1964; Lipner 1986

Prakara: according to *Nyaya,* a complex cognition is true when its structured content (*vishayata*) corresponds to its external object (*visheshya*) as it is actually characterised by its properties (*visheshana*). The components of the mental content are called *prakara*. **Ramanuja** applies the term to any entity that essentially depends upon something else.

Prakashatman (900–75 CE): *Advaita-Vedantin* author of the *Pancapadika-vivarana* who held that the underlying cause of experienced diversity is **Brahman** qualified by a power of cosmic ignorance called **maya** or **avidya**. This force is neither real nor unreal (*anirvacaniya*). But it is a positive entity (*bhava-rupa*) since it differs from the mere prior absence of knowledge or blank ignorance.

Against the view of *Vachaspati Mishra* that the Abso-lute (*Brahman*) is the object of *avidya* and the limited self its substrate, he held that *Brahman* is both the substrate and object of *avidya*. Oppositions between differentiated subjects, acts and objects of cognition are superimposed upon immutable, self-luminous pure consciousness. So the whole of reality – subjects, objects and experiences – is a gigantic mistake. But it is an error about something, namely, the nature of ultimate reality. Were it otherwise, the conclusion would follow that reality is emptiness (*shunyata*).

Further reading: Bartley 2002; Gerow 1990

Pralaya (cosmic retraction): Hindu religious cults understand the cosmos as being emitted from and reabsorbed into an underlying causal substrate. During reabsorption bodies, faculties and basic material elements exist in a potential state. Souls who have not been liberated are also reab-sorbed with their accumulated *karma*-stock, which influ-ences the general conditions of their rebirth.

Prama (knowledge or true cognition): to count as a piece of knowledge a cognition must have been produced by a re-liable method (*pramana*), and correspond to some reality, whether the object be an aspect of the physical world or something mental (if you are an idealist believing that only thoughts are real). Most philosophers accept that our perceptual and inferential processes are basically re-liable and that cognitions can be assumed to be true until they are explicitly contradicted. Truth is manifested in successful activity, but it is not the same as pragmatic success. The stipulation that knowledge yields new infor-mation means that a memory does not count as knowl-edge, although it may be true. A memory is true only if its originating experience was.

The later *Nyaya* realist philosophers analyse the object of cognition into some subject (*visheshya*) that has a property (*visheshana*), the two being held together by a relation. An experience is true when the structure of its content (*vishayata*) mirrors or corresponds to that of the objective situation. Error most typically occurs when the modifier in the cognition (*prakara* corresponding to the *visheshana* in the object) is not actually related to the subject in the current perceptual situation.

Further reading: G. Bhattacharya 1989; Matilal 2002b; Mohanty 1966 and 1992

Pramana: a reliable method for gaining knowledge. The majority of Indian philosophers recognise sense perception (*pratyaksha*), inference (*anumana*) and verbal testimony (*shabda*) as *pramanas* in their own right. Most hold that beliefs are justified and true if they are formed by a process that generally produces true beliefs. (For example, perceptual beliefs are justified if they come about via sensory stimulation from objects in the environment. They are not justified if they are produced by hallucination, which is not a reliable mechanism.) *Kumarila*'s view (in which he is followed by most *Vedanta* thinkers) that a *pramana* provides new information by revealing something previously not known to be the case was very influential. The primary reliable instrument of knowledge is sensory perception. Information from perception supplies the data for inferences. Testimony includes the word of experts and whatever one accepts as scripture. The materialist *Carvakas* accept only sense perception; Buddhists accept only perception and inference; the *Samkhyas* accept perception, inference and testimony; the *Naiyayikas* accept perception, inference, testimony and comparison (*upamana*); the *Prabhakaras* in the **Purva Mimamsa** tradition accept perception, inference, testimony, comparison and presumption (*arthapatti*); the *Mimamsaka* followers of **Kumarila** accept perception, inference, testimony, comparison, presumption and noncognition (*anupalabdhi*). The Buddhist anti-realist sceptic **Nagarjuna** asks how we establish the validity of the pramanas that are supposed to establish the nature of objects. If we say that they do not need to be established, why do we think that objects need *pramanas* for their determination? But if we say that a *pramana* is established by another *pramana*, an infinite regress (*anavastha*) results.

Further reading: G. Bhattacharya 1989; K. Bhattacharya 1998; Franco 1994; Matilal 1986; Potter 1977; Suryanarayana Shastri 1942

Pramana-samplava (co-extensivity of the means of knowledge): realists, especially the **Nyaya-Vaisheshikas** and **Purva Mimamsakas**, oppose the view of the **Sautrantika** Buddhists that conceptual thought and language are human constructions only indirectly related to the inexpressible, momentary real particulars (*svalakshana*) that are given only in perceptual sensation. They hold that our concepts, simple and complex, correspond to, by way of copying, reality as it is actually structured. Both individual entities and their properties are objective realities and may be known by sensory perception (*nirvikalpaka-pratyaksha*), concept-laden perception (*savikalpaka-pratyaksha*) and inference (*anumana*). Fire may be known by both perception and inference, as when its presence is deduced from that of smoke.

See **Pramana-vyavastha**

Pramana-vyavastha: while the realists hold that, for instance, fire as a whole concrete reality may either be perceived by more than one of the senses, or grasped by inference, the Buddhist view is that the visual sense grasps only colour, the tactile sense grasps only heat, the auditory sense grasps only crackling, and the sense of smell grasps burning. Moreover, the two reliable means of knowledge (sense perception or *pratyaksha* and inference or *anumana*) exclusively have their own domains. No entity of a certain type can be the object of two different *pramanas*. What is perceivable is not inferable and vice versa. The unique, inexpressible particulars that are given in sensory perceptions cannot be the direct objects of awareness involving conceptual construction. This means that if there is a mind-independent reality, it is literally unthinkable. Concepts, such as those of fire and smoke, are products of conceptualisation (*vikalpa*; *kalpana*) operating on sensory impressions (or, for the idealist *Vijnanavada*, complexes of simple ideas). Inferences involving smoke and fire operate at this conceptual level, which is indirectly related to the temporary combinations of particular instants.

Acceptance of this view means that the Buddhist cannot know how many reliable means of knowledge there are. If a cognition is not grasped by another cognition but only by itself, and if perception is grasped only by perception and inference only by inference, and if there is no persisting soul that could coordinate different cognitions, then one cannot count the reliable means of knowledge.

Pramanya (the veridicality of knowledge): it is a controversial issue whether when one knows something one must also explicitly know that one knows. Does having a true thought require that one knows its truth? Can we be said to know without subjective certainty? The theory that the conditions that produce cognition are sufficient to produce its truth (*prama*) is the view that truthfulness is intrinsic to knowledge (*svatah pramanya*). The theory

that the causal conditions of a cognition are not sufficient for its being true, which requires some extra confirmatory factor, is the view that truthfulness is extrinsic
to knowledge (*paratah pramanya*). After *Dharmakirti*,
most Buddhist philosophers say that some cognitions are
true intrinsically and others extrinsically, according to circumstances.

Further reading: G. Bhattacharya 1989; Matilal 2002b;
Mohanty 1966 and 1992

Prasajya-pratishedha (verbally-bound or propositional negation): the term signifying negation is connected with the
verb and there is no positive implication. For example,
'Do not eat garlic' does not tell one what to eat and 'Don't
look at the sun' does not tell one what to look at.

Some *Madhyamaka Buddhists* appeal to this form of
negation: they can reject opposing views without attract-
ing the objection that they are guilty of self-contradiction
by implicitly committing themselves to a dogmatic position or just a positive truth-claim.

See *Paryudasa-pratishedha*

Prasanga (unwanted consequence; reduction to the absurd):
an argumentative technique that takes into consideration
the opposite to what is actually believed and demon-
strates that it leads to unwanted consequences. The belief
is thereby validated. A Buddhist would argue:

Suppose that an entity has an unchanging nature.
Suppose that it is capable of causal activity.
It is always capable of exercising that causal activity.
So in the present, it is producing past and future
effects.

In other cases, the technique is deployed to demonstrate that an opponent's position, in its own terms, is

inconsistent. And, bearing in mind that, for the *Nyaya* school, universals are simple and have many instances:

Whatever occurs in many instances must be complex.
A universal is held to occur in many instances.
It must be complex.

Further reading: Kajiyama 1998; Matilal 1986 and 2002b

Pratitya-samutpada (interdependent origination): the basic Buddhist theory that sees causality as nothing more than one thing's always following another in our experience. Events occur successively but there are no real causal relations or forces over and above what happens. What we interpret as cause and effect cannot be joined by a real relation that is a further factor since cause and effect occur at different times. Dependent origination is also the rejection of the view that there are types of individual entities with innate and specific causal powers: acorns don't contain tiny oak trees in a state of potentiality. But it also denies that things happen randomly, which would make nonsense of moral responsibility. Anything recognised as an entity has come into being in dependence on a complex of conditions. Buddhists deny that there are any singular persisting entities that produce others. Rather, reality consists of cooperating moments in fields of energies that are held together by a sort of magnetism. The latter power imposes temporary continuity on a stream of events. Individual people are streams of such essentially temporary physical and mental factors. The theory of conditioned origination is an attempt to account for our experience of organisation and repeatability. It applies to the physical and psychological realms and guarantees that actions will produce consequences appropriate to their moral quality.

It is a structuring principle that automatically governs the formations and interactions of the basic mental and physical elements of existence (*dharma*). Morality requires such organisation because Buddhists deny that there is any persisting entity such as the soul (*atman*) that would link thoughts and actions with their results in this and future lives and which would experience the consequences of ethically significant actions (*karma*). And there is no God who could act as a moral superintendent.

Interdependent origination is sometimes expressed as a twelvefold chain: basic ignorance (*avidya*) conditions karmic dispositions (*samskara*), which condition mental events (*vijnana*), which condition the psycho-physical body (*nama-rupa*), which conditions the sensory receptors, which condition sense–object interactions, which condition feelings (*vedana*), which condition 'thirst' or desire, which conditions craving (*upadana*), which conditions repeated existences (*bhava*), which condition births (*jati*), which condition old age and death (*jara-maranam*) and all our woe.

The *Madhyamaka* school, founded by *Nagarjuna*, interprets *pratitya-samutpada* in terms of the relativity of all conditioned things.

See *Satkaryavada* and *Asatkaryavada*

Further reading: Collins 1982; Gethin 1998; Rahula 1969

Pratiyogin (counterpart of an absence or the absentee): when I see that the keys are not on the desk, my mental image of the missing keys is the counterpart of the perceived absence. *Nyaya-Vaisheshika* philosophers define an effect as the counterpart of its prior absence.

Further reading: Matilal 1968

Pratyabhijna ('Recognition'): Kashmiri school of philosophy connected with a monistic form of Shiva worship.

Original thinkers include *Somananda* (900–50 CE), *Utpaladeva* (925–75 CE) and *Abhinavagupta* (975–1025 CE) who teach a form of absolute idealism according to which everything that appears to us as material and everything individual is projected by a single consciousness. The argument is that whatever causes the physical world must be non-physical. Since individual centres of consciousness are localised by matter, the ultimate source must be unconditioned, creative universal consciousness. On the individual level, we can only make sense of the coherence of our experiences and memories if they belong to a single persisting conscious subject (inhabiting a stable world regulated by objective structures). This is extended macrocosmically. The universe of subjects and objects holds together because it has a single conscious source that preserves it in being. The coordination of diverse subjects and objects is possible only if they are aspects of a single, universal field of experience. Universal Consciousness causes objects of awareness to appear as if distinct from the limited subjects of experience. The forms figuring in our awareness have as their objects the ideas (*abhasa*) projected by the universal consciousness.

The goal of religious practice is the transcendence of limited individual subjectivity. Enlightenment is the realisation that the subject that has selfishly considered itself as an individual is identical with the universal transcendental conscious energy (*samvit*), named *Shiva*. Liberation from rebirth (*moksha*) is the recognition that, 'I am Shiva and this whole world is my self-expression'. The authentic identity is already present as the constant background to all experience but must be re-cognised and reflected upon as the ultimate conscious principle manifesting itself as all limited subjects, acts and objects of experience. What appear as external, physical objects depend upon consciousness. Since causality is exclusively a property of conscious agents capable of volition, creativity by the physical is impossible. Since only an idea can be like and thus represent an idea, consciousness would not represent matter if matter were something totally different from it. We cannot experience anything other than consciousness.

Further reading: Singh 1982; Torella 2002

Pratyaksha-anupalambha (positive and negative perceptions): the Buddhist *Dharmakirti* thinks that a causal connection (*karya-karana-bhava*) is one of the two forms of natural regularity (*svabhava-pratibandha*) between the logical reason and what is to be proved in a formal inference. A causal relation is understood through positive and negative perceptions. The causal connection between smoke and fire is known when we find that smoke, which had not been present, appears when fire is introduced and that, when the fire is extinguished, the smoke disappears.

This is applied in a proof of the existence of streams of experience other than one's own. Given that we see that our own actions happen after our intentions and that they do not happen in the absence of our intentions, there is a causal connection between intention and the occurrence of action. The causal relation is established by perception and non-perception and consists in positive and negative agreement. Seeing that actions separate from us occur even when we have not framed any intention, we infer intentions elsewhere to be the cause of the other actions. Thus other minds are established.

Pratyaksha-pramana (sense perception as a reliable method of acquiring knowledge): the *Nyaya* tradition says that perception is a cognitive episode arising from contact between some object and a sense organ. It is non-verbal, reliable and determinate. Most *Nyaya* thinkers accept that the relation is a physical one in accordance with their view that cognition is always the manifestation of some object belonging to the physical environment. They take it for granted that sensory perception is our basic mode of acquiring knowledge. The Buddhist *Dignaga* distinguishes sharply between two types of mental process: perception, which is free from conceptual interpretation and language, and mental construction (*vikalpa/kalpana*). The former relates directly to reality – a flux of inexpressible, momentary particulars: the latter organises that flux of instants under general concepts and is thus at one remove from the data of experience. *Dignaga* denies that perceptual experiences can be expressed in words. They are thus incommunicable. This disjunction is resisted by the *Nyaya* thinkers and those influenced by them. They hold that some reliable perceptions involve concepts and are linguistically expressible (*savikalpaka-pratyaksha*), while others are concept free (*nirvikalpaka-pratyaksha*).

Further reading: G. Bhattacharya 1989; Franco 1994; Matilal 1986; Mohanty 1992; Potter 1977

Pratyaya (four causal factors): *Abhidharma* Buddhists, who think that the primary data of awareness are provided by realities external to the mind, analyse events as complexes (*samagri*) comprising four types of causal conditions: a preceding moment in any sort of series is called the immediate condition (*samanantara-pratyaya*); an object-condition (*alambana-pratyaya*); an efficient condition (*adhipati-pratyaya*); and attendant circumstantial conditions (*hetu-pratyaya*). A perception such as that of the colour red would be analysed as a complex event:

1. The immediately preceding moment in the stream of consciousness (*samanantara-pratyaya*).
2. A flash of red atoms (*alambana-pratyaya* or objective condition).

3. An operation of the visual faculty (*adhipati-pratyaya*).
4. Light (*hetu-pratyaya*).

Buddhist *Sautrantikas*, who deny that we are directly in touch with objective reality consisting of an elusive flux of instantaneous unique particulars (*svalakshana*) and think that our ideas are the primary objects of awareness, say that the *alambana-pratyaya* is the red mental image that the mind forms after sensory perception of the fleeting realities. This immediately preceding perception is the *samanantara-pratyaya*. They rename the *hetu-pratyaya* as the *sahakari-pratyaya*. It becomes the cooperation between the two different sorts of consciousness: pure sensation and image formation.

The Buddhist idealists (**Vijnanavada**) think that only ideas exist and that minds have a tendency to project them as if they were external things. They see no need to postulate the existence of real material atoms. They say that an idea occurring in a stream can be the objective ground of another idea. An idea with red content becomes the object of another idea.

Further reading: Frauwallner 1995; Kajiyama 1998; Stcherbatsky 1993

Pudgalavada (Personalist theory): there were some early Buddhists (*Vatsiputriyas* or *Sammitiyas*) who, while not accepting the soul (*atman*) as a further fact over and above the stream of experiences, thought that there was an entity called a person (*pudgala*) that emerged from the interactions of the five constituents (*skandhas*: body, feelings, perceptions, dispositions of character and thoughts) with which it was neither identical nor distinct. It could neither be classified as an ultimate reality, nor as a purely fictional invention. The motivation for this view was probably that constituents of personality and their combinations were insufficiently substantial to be the bearer of moral responsibility and the recipient of the future consequences of actions. This view was rejected by most Buddhists as a surreptitious return of the notion of soul or permanent identity.

Further reading: Conze 1959; Mookerjee 1975

Purusha the *Samkhya* concept of soul (*atman*). There is an infinite number of self-contained and isolated centres of radiant but inactive blank consciousness. When entangled in matter (*prakriti*), these monads are merely the witnesses of thoughts and feelings that are properties of the basically material intellect.

Purushartha: in Hinduism, the legitimate goals of human life were initially conceived as social and religious duty (*dharma*), from which flows economic prosperity (*artha*), which is a consequence of the householder's following his proper occupation, and sensual pleasure (*kama*) whose ultimate aim is procreation. This formulation prescribes what a man must do if he is to live in harmony with natural law and thus help to perpetuate the universal cosmic order. To these were added final liberation (*moksha*) from bondage to rebirth as an individual in the here and now (*samsara*). This is effectively the rejection of the other three values. But the conception was successfully integrated into the dominant ideology by specifying *moksha* as the *dharma* of the renouncer (*samnyasin*) who had fulfilled his duties as a member of the shared public religion. This negative form of duty was termed *nivritti-dharma* ('religion of renunciation') in contradistinction to active religion (*pravritti-dharma*) of the ordinary householder in the world. The tension between the two is sometimes seen as one of the enduring features of Hinduism.

Further reading: Flood 1996

Purva Mimamsa/Purva Mimamsaka: one of the six mainstream Hindu *darshanas*, this is systematic reflection upon the meaning and fruits of ritual religion prescribed by those portions of the eternal, authorless and infallible *Vedas* that are the only source of knowledge (*pramana*) about social and religious duty. They insist that the purpose of the *Veda* is to tell the qualified Hindu what actions have to be performed. The *Mimamsaka* outlook was not theistic in that they believed that the gods (*devas*) existed only in name, only in so far as their names were mentioned in the sacrificial rituals. They maintained that the universe is beginningless and that its continued existence depended upon the Vedic rituals and not upon divine creation and support. The cosmos is a self-regulating process, the arena in which sentient beings perform actions and reap their consequences.

Exact performance being necessary for the ritual's success, precise understanding of the instructions was essential. This lead to a concern with the nature and operation of words and sentences. They claim that the relation between a word and its object is innate (*autpattika*) and permanent (*nitya*). The word–meaning relation holds between the word's sound and the form (*akriti*) common to the class of objects that it denotes. Word sounds participate in the nature of their objects.

The need to establish the infallible authority of the *Veda* led them into enquiries into the scope of the means of knowledge (*pramana*). *Mimamsakas* say that the mind is a blank slate, passively receiving data. Cognitions are acts that manifest a mind-independent external world. As such, they may be presumed always valid. So the authority of the *Vedic* commands is unquestionable simply because they are known.

The basic text is the *Mimamsa Sutra* of *Jaimini* (c. 100 CE) with the commentary by *Shabara* (fourth century CE).

In the second half of the seventh century the school divided into the followers of *Kumarila* and *Prabhakara*, the latter insisting that the *Vedic* injunctions (*vidhi*) incite action automatically, while the former hold that their motivating force is the prospect of rewards yielded by the rituals. Ritual performance keeps the cosmos going, provides benefits in this life and heavenly pleasures (*svarga*) for those who acquire sufficient merit. The developed tradition understands the soul as in itself an eternal spiritual essence that is embodied owing to *karma* and which really becomes involved in active life. The disinterested performance of ritual in a spirit of 'duty for duty's sake' effects a depersonalisation, culminating in release from rebirth once one's *karma* stock has been exhausted.

The *Vedic* statements are classified as action commands (*vidhi*), descriptions and explanations (*arthavada*), and incantations (*mantra*) to be used in the rituals. Since the *Veda* teaches what must be done in the ritual sphere, action commands are primary. *Arthavadas* are auxiliary statements that motivate the performance of actions commanded by *vidhis* by stating their rewards.

Further reading: Cowell and Gough 1996; Hiriyanna 1993; Jha 1964 and 1964

Purvavat: the inference of an effect from a cause. We may infer some future event on the basis of a present one, as when we predict rain from clouds.

Ramakantha Bhatta (950–1000 CE): principal philosopher of the dualistic and realistic Kashmiri *Shaiva Siddhanta*

ritual cult. His works include the *Nareshvaraparik-shaprakasha* and commentaries on the *Matangaparame-shavara Agama* and the *Kiranatantra* as well as commentaries on works by *Sadyojyoti*.

His principal opponents include Buddhists in the tradition of **Dignaga** and **Dharmakirti,** some of whose theories had been translated into a metaphysic of absolute idealism by **Utpaladeva** who belonged to the rival Kashmiri Shaiva **Pratyabhijna** school.

He defends the view that individual souls are permanent centres of knowledge and agency. Individual thinking subjects are basic realities in the sense that, while tables and chairs need observers to establish their identities, souls need no external establishment. He refutes the Buddhist view that we are just streams of experiences superimposing continuity upon themselves, maintaining that the persisting identity and responsible agency of the soul is self-evident to each individual and pointing out the disastrous implications for human behaviour were it accepted that the one who performs the deed is other than the one who experiences its results. This involves a refutation of the Buddhist repudiation of real structures of causes and effects in favour of the mere occurrence of successive events. He also criticises forms of Buddhist idealism in defending the *Siddhantin* belief that we experience a real objective environment that has been created by God. He thinks that the existence of God can be proved by inference: the world consists of composite realities; whatever is composite has a conscious maker adequate to its complexity.

Further reading: Goodall 1998; Sanderson 1992

Ramanuja (fl. 1100 CE): *Ramanuja* was a theologian of theistic **Vedanta** resolutely opposed to the non-dualist (*advaita*) traditions. He wanted to show that the beliefs and practices of his devotional *Shri Vaishnava* cult were the true expression of the orthodox *Vedic* religion represented by the **Brahma-Sutras**, the **Upanishads**, the **Bhagavad Gita** and the **Dharmashastra** literature. His most important works are the commentary on the **Brahma-Sutras**, called the *Shri Bhashya*, the commentary on the **Bhagavad Gita** and the 'Compendium of the Meaning of the Scriptures' (*Vedarthasamgraha*).

While the *Advaitins* view the world including individual experiencers and agents as an illusion concealing an impersonal Absolute that is inactive, featureless consciousness, Ramanuja sees it as really created by a personal God who invites our loving response. He believes that there are three types of realities: a personal divine life called *Vishnu Narayana*; individual souls which are always aware of their enduring identities whether they be subject to **karma** or enjoying the supernatural state that is exempt from **karma**; and physical bodies and objects occupying the material environment. Souls and matter depend upon God: a physical body is an entity only if there is a soul associated with it. Interpreting some passages in the **Upanishads**, which refer to a soul who is the inner self and guide (*antaryamin*) of individual selves, he articulates the relation between God and the world of souls and matter in a soul–body model (*sharira-shariri-bhava*). He accepts the **satkaryavada** theory of causation according to which effects pre-exist in their underlying cause before becoming entities. **Brahman** is called the cause of the universe when its body is in its causal mode, 'containing' all entities in potential form. **Brahman** is in its effected mode when selves and matter are manifested. Theorists belonging to the **Bheda-abheda-vada** tradition thought that creation is a transformation of God (*Brahma-parinama-vada*). For *Ramanuja* this implied too close an association between God and the cosmos. His view is that the creation of the cosmos occurs in the sphere of **Brahman**'s body and does not affect the divine life as it is in itself.

Ramanuja understands devotion to God (*bhakti*) as a mode of relationship with the personal god *Vishnu Narayana* that will culminate in communion with god in heaven. Devotion is more than feeling. It involves the awareness of one's ultimate dependence upon God, the inner guide. In this world, devotion is expressed in the unselfish observation of one's *caste*-based social and religious duties (*varna-ashrama-dharma*). It is a response to a profound conviction that if God is the foundational cause of everything, then everything one does is also an action of God. This does not mean that one's actions are not one's own. It means that it is thanks to God's initiative that the dependent soul is itself an entity with its own activity.

See *Lila*

Further reading: Bartley 2002; Buitenen 1953 and 1956; Carman 1974; Cowell and Gough 1996; Lipner 1986; Thibaut 1904a

S

Saccidananda (Being–Consciousness–Delight): this is an *Advaita-Vedantin* expression for the Authentic Reality (*Brahman*). The true reality is unconditioned self-awareness delighting in itself. It is a state of pure tranquillity, beyond all oppositions such as that between knower and known. This is perhaps what the introverted mediator, who has renounced the world of change with all it objects of attachment, frustrations and anxieties, experiences in profound states of contemplation. His experience of unity and peace tells him that the world of differences, change and becoming cannot be truly real. It is a poor substitute for the unalloyed bliss of tranquil absorption in pure consciousness.

Undifferentiated being is equated with consciousness. Consciousness is foundational in that it can never be negated. Only something conscious can ask questions about the nature of consciousness. While the existence of entities is established by consciousness, consciousness is self-established, needing nothing outside itself. Whatever is an object of consciousness can be negated. It is because consciousness cannot be negated that it is authentic Being.

Sadharmya-drishtanta see *Hetu* and *Sapaksha*

Sadhya: in the context of an inference (*anumana*; *prayoga*), that which is sought to be established or the object to be inferred. Typically, the inference begins with a doubt about the occurrence of the *sadhya* in the subject of the inference. Is there fire on the mountain? Yes, because there is smoke (*hetu*). Smoke is said to be pervaded by fire: wherever there is smoke, there is fire. The relationship between smoke and fire is one of invariable association (*vyapti*).

Further reading: G. Bhattacharya 1989; Ganeri 2001b

Saguna Brahman: the view of theistic *Vedantins* such as *Ramanuja* and *Madhva* that the ultimate foundation of reality (*Brahman*) is a personal God that is both creatively active and endowed with super-eminent qualities such as being all-powerful, all-knowing and blissful. Such a God responds favourably to human devotion.

Sahopalambha-niyama (invariable co-apprehension): this is an argument that we can attach no sense to the notion of physical reality existing apart from minds. Since the awareness of blue is simultaneous with the blue thing, and blue and the awareness of blue never occur separately, we must assume that they are the same. As interpreted by in the Buddhist idealist *Vijnanavada*, this means that that there is nothing external to minds. As interpreted by *Sautrantikas* like *Dharmakirti*, it means that we only know our ideas and that we cannot know reality as it is in itself outside the mind.

Sakara-vada: this is a Buddhist view that each object-awareness has its own form or mental image (*akara*) that distinguishes it from other ideas. The form is what we are directly aware of and think with. It may derive from some extra-mental reality of which we have received sensory impressions, or it may just be an idea. The former is the view of the *Sautrantikas* and the latter that of the idealist *Vijnanavadins* who hold that everyday unenlightened experience is just consciousness projecting its forms in such a way that they appear to be external objects. From the presence of forms in awareness, *Sautrantikas* infer an objective domain that causes them. But since we only know our ideas, we can never be acquainted with whatever causes them.

All Buddhist idealists agreed that the awareness of the enlightened person is free from the distinction between object and cognising subject. But some thought that it is also free from images that are necessarily features of unenlightened experience. They call this *Nirakara-vada*, an expression that usually labels the view that consciousness is a formless light illuminating a ready-made world of objects.

See *Dharmakirti*

Further reading: Kajiyama 1998; Matilal 1986

Samanadhikaranya: in logic, *samanadhikaranya* means co-occurrence of two or more items (for example, an individual substance and its properties) in the same substrate. In grammatical usage, it means the reference to one object by terms that have different grounds for their application (*pravritti-nimitta*). The interpretation of co-referential *Upanishadic* statements such as *Tat tvam asi* ('That thou art') and *Satyam jnanam anantam brahma* ('The Supreme Being is Reality, Consciousness, Infinite') is central to *Vedantic* theology. Non-dualistic **Advaita Vedantins** such as **Shankara** emphasise the singleness of reference and take co-referential constructions as identity statements conveying a featureless essence. So the different grounds for the applications of the terms are treated as modes of presentation that the mind can grasp. *Ramanuja* and his followers hold that the differences between the grounds for the applications of the words imply objective distinctions in what they are about. *Samanadhikaranya* is thus the reference to one object of words expressing several properties that the entity actually possesses.

Further reading: Bartley 2002

Samanya (generic property) or **jati** (natural kind): according to *Nyaya-Vaisheshika* one of the types of basic features of the cosmos (*padartha*). These are objectively real general properties inhering in substantial continuants (*dravya*), qualities (*guna*) and motions (*karman*). They are unitary, eternal and present in many particular entities (*vyakti*). Structural principles organising the natural world, they explain why a given general term or concept can be applied to a number of distinct individuals. They account for our awareness of common features. Universals are hierarchically ordered. Being (*satta*), present in all substances, qualities and motions, is the most inclusive. Next come substance-ness, quality-ness and action-ness. Then there are the properties shared by natural kinds and artefacts: cowness, treeness, potness and clothness. (What are artefacts from a human point of view can be treated as quasi-natural configurations since they are causally related to physical atoms.) These are manifested in the concrete physical structure (*akriti* or *samsthana*) common to a kind. Universals are shared by tokens of types of particular properties (*guna*) and actions (*karman*). All red instances have redness in common. The same applies to the five types of motions.

Universals regulate generative causality in that they impose limits on difference and change. An entity cannot change into another of a different kind. But an entity can become another (natural reproduction) just in case the same universal occurs in each.

Neither every shared characteristic is an objective universal, nor do all general terms stand for them.

See *jati-badhaka* and *upadhi*

Further reading: G. Bhattacharya 1989; Potter 1977

Samanya-lakshana (extraordinary perception): in *Nyaya-Vaisheshika* this means perception of the universal property common to all members of a class, although only one of the members is present to the mind. It also means that although no one has observed every case of smoke and every case of fire, their invariable association can be known. When we use an inference of the form: 'There is fire on the mountain. Because there is smoke on the mountain. Wherever there is smoke there is fire: Like in the kitchen', the *Nyaya* philosopher says that once one has seen the association of smoke and fire in the kitchen, one understands through extraordinary perception both the universals smokeness and fireness and the relationship of pervasion (*vyapti*) between them. Since the universals occur in all cases of smoke and fire, it follows that one perceives the pervasion that holds in all cases, including the mountain.

Samanyato-drishta: a type of inference accepted by *Nyaya-Vaisheshika* and *Samkhya*. It is used to infer what can never be perceived (for example, self, space, time, atoms and the primal material cause) by the senses. It works like this: observation that a body has changed its place implies movement. If I see a star at two different positions in the night sky, I may infer that it moves although the movement is imperceptible.

If qualities always belong to substrates and if desire and cognition are qualities, I can infer that there is a self to which they belong.

Samavaya (inherence): according to *Nyaya-Vaisheshika* this relation is one of the basic types of reality (*padartha*). *Nyaya* posits a universe consisting of innumerable objects and structuring factors. Continuing substances, particular qualities, movements and universal properties are all counted as entities. There has to be a sort of relation that can combine such realities into complexes while preserving the differences between types. *Samavaya* is the relation by which types are held together while retaining their own identities. It is the cement of the universe. It integrates the constituents comprising particular objects. It combines two items when one is inseparable from the other in the sense that the breaking of the connection entails the destruction of one of the terms. It thus differs from conjunction (*samyoga* – which links individual substances), where both terms survive separation.

Inherence obtains between particular qualities (*guna*) and the substances possessing them, actions and their substrates, universals and their particular instances, and individuators (*vishesha*) and the permanent substances (for example, souls and atoms) that they uniquely specify by inhering therein.

A complex substance is a whole (*avayavin*) inhering in each of its parts. A cloth cannot continue in existence without the threads, while the threads may exist separately. Qualities and action inhere in substances. The particular case of the quality blue that is a feature of some lotus needs the lotus for its occurrence. A quality is always a property *of* something. Although *we* never encounter a lotus without some quality or other, at the first moment of its existence, the substance has neither qualities nor actions. Quality presupposes substance but substance does not presuppose quality. Qualities (and actions) only exist in some substance that supports them.

Universals inhere in substances, qualities and motions. An individual cow is nothing unless it is an instance of the generic property cowness.

It may appear that if x and y are joined by R and R is also a reality, we will need further connections to relate R to x and R to y. This would generate an infinite series of relations. To avoid this, the tradition holds that inherence relates itself to its terms – it behaves like glue.

Further reading: G. Bhattacharya 1989; Halbfass 1992; Potter 1977

Samkhya: one of the six orthodox Hindu systems of salvation (*Darshana*), usually associated with the **Yoga** tradition. The school's basic text is the *Samkhya Karikas* of Ishvarakrishna (c. 400–500 CE) upon which there are commentaries among which are the *Yuktidipika* (c. 650 CE) and **Vachaspati Mishra**'s *Tattvakaumudi* (c. 841 or 976 CE). *Samkhya*, a world-renunciatory outlook, posits a dualism of souls (*Purusha* – an infinity of isolated, inactive spirits outside space and time) and Primal Matter (*Pradhana* or *Mula Prakriti*) that transforms itself (*parinama*) into the cosmos of mental and material phenomena. They accept the *satkaryavada* theory of causation which holds that products pre-exist in a potential form in their underlying, material causes. Prime Matter consists of three strands or qualities (*guna*): *sattva* (goodness and light), *rajas* (dynamic energy) and *tamas* (heavy and dark). Before the cosmic transformation, they are in a state of equilibrium, cancelling out one another's properties. The *Purushas* are inactive, individual centres of unchanging self-awareness. Their 'mere existence' is said to prompt the transformation of material nature. *Prakriti* transforms for the sake of the human souls so that they have experiences that lead them to realise the difference between soul and matter. Opponents ask how an unconscious cause can act for the sake of anything, let alone produce specific and organised realities.

Matter evolves to produce the basic material and psychological realities (*tattva* – *buddhi* (mind); *ahamkara* (ego and will); *manas* (sensory coordinator); the five senses (*indriya*), physical organs; the essences of sounds, touch, colours, tastes and smells; and the gross elements – space, air, fire, water and earth which make up physical objects). These products contain the *gunas* in differing proportions.

The *Purushas* become entangled in and misidentify themselves with aspects of the material environment, in particular psychological faculties and body. Given the 'proximity' of the *Purusha*-consciousness to the mind (*buddhi*), the latter is illuminated (the material *buddhi* becomes 'consciousness-like') and the confusion is compounded when the activity of the *buddhi* is misattributed to the inactive *Purusha*. Thus we have the origins of the individual person and the series of births marked by suffering. Liberation (*kaivalya* – 'wholeness', 'isola-tion') from the *samsaric* cycle of unsatisfactory becom-ing results from the discriminating insight, presupposing the discipline of **Yoga**, that the conscious principle is dis-tinct from the physical and psychological sphere. *Prakriti* ceases to function in relation to the enlightened spirit. Liberation occurs when the *gunas* are reabsorbed into *prakriti*. The soul recovers its true form, detached from mental modifications.

Some *Samkhya* thinkers accepted the existence of God, who is pure awareness, without asserting that he either creates or is involved in the domain of souls and matter.

Further reading: Hiriyanna 1993; Larson 1979; Larson and Bhattacharya 1987

Samkhya (number): numbers are classified by the **Vaisheshikas** as one of the sub-varieties of the category (*padartha*) quality (*guna*). A quality is a non-repeatable particular property. The particular grey belonging to the sky outside is different from, although belonging to the same type as, the grey of my hair. Qualities can only be properties of substances (*dravya*). In the case of number we can say that every object has a unit-quality distinct from but of the same kind as every other unit-quality. The quality 'two' inheres in each member of a pair and 'three' in each of a triad, and so on. But because numbers are qualities, the **Vaisheshika** system does not let us ascribe a number to a multiplicity of qualities (although we can count the objects in which the quality inheres). In response to this problem, the **Nyaya** philoso-pher **Bhasarvajna** denies that numbers are qualities and understands them in terms of identity and difference. To say that something is one (or that there is one of something) is just to assert the entity's identity. Saying two and so on is asserting difference.

The *Navya-Nyaya* philosopher *Raghunatha* argues that number is a separate category of reality (*padartha*), not a variety of quality, because we ascribe number to qualities. Numbers apply to objects in a way different from that in which universals and qualities do. A number applies to a group (for example, eleven footballers) collectively. It is not related distributively to each member (as when we say, 'the birds are singing' we mean that each bird is singing) because it is not the case that each member of the team is eleven. The relation of a number to a collection is of a unique type that he calls 'comprehension' (*paryapti*). The attribution of number depends upon the mind counting and grouping individuals. This does not mean that numbers are subjective impositions: two exists and we perceive pairs, three exists and we perceive triads.

Further reading: G. Bhattacharya 1989; Ganeri 2001a; Ingalls 1951; Matilal 2002b

Samnyasa (renunciation of social and religious duty): the renunciation of ritual religion and caste status. It is formalised through a special type of initiation ritual. Initially this may have been an expression of the endless repetitions characterising the everyday life of the adult male householder with his duties of wealth creation, procreation and the performance and patronage of rituals. But it was integrated into mainstream religion and classified as the fourth stage of life (*ashrama*) additional to those of celibate studentship, being a householder (*grihastha*) and retirement or 'forest-dwelling' (*vanaprastha*). The ideal of ultimate liberation (*moksha*) from the series of births was sometimes defined as the duty (*svadharma*) of the renouncer. It is accepted that detached and self-controlled individuals of unusual virtue may renounce without having lived as householders.

Renouncers are homeless wanderers committed to celibacy. They possess only a saffron robe, begging bowl and staff. They are dedicated to liberation from rebirth through insight (*jnana-marga*) into the nature of the soul. The *Advaita-Vedantin* thinker **Shankara**, himself a renouncer, thinks that the rituals and their results belong to the sphere of ignorance and desire and have no place in the life of the person who has realised that the soul is identical with the supreme reality beyond all difference and change.

Nevertheless, renunciation has always been controversial and for some people renouncers are objects of fear and suspicion. There is a resistance to the idea that anyone should abandon the rituals commanded by the **Vedas** and go it alone. So some traditions hold that ritual performance is mandatory: what one should renounce is desire for the results of the rituals.

Further reading: Dumont 1980; Olivelle 1986

Samsara: the unsatisfactory round of embodied existences propelled by the accumulated stock of merit and demerit (*karma*) associated with the soul (*atman*) and by which it is personalised. Release (*moksha*) from rebirth is the ultimate goal of all paths to salvation.

See *Duhkha*

Samyoga (relation of conjunction): conjunction is classified by the **Vaisheshikas** as one of the sub-varieties of the category (*padartha*) quality (*guna*). This relation obtains only between individual substances (*dravya*). Direct conjunction, or contact between the surfaces of objects, is produced by some action. It is a separable relation, each case of which lasts as long as things are linked.

While the threads that have been woven to make a whole cloth are held together by inherence (*samavaya*), a heap of threads is related by conjunction.

Further reading: G. Bhattacharya 1989; Halbfass 1992; Potter 1977

Sapaksha: in an inference, an instance other than the subject (*paksha*) that has both the property to be proved (*sadhya*) and the logical reason or proving property (*hetu*). It exemplifies and supports a law such as, 'Wherever there is smoke, there is fire.' There, the *sapaksha* could be the kitchen.

Further reading: G. Bhattacharya 1989; Ganeri 2001b; Tillemans 1999

Sarvastivada see *Vaibhashika*

Satkaryavada (theory that effects pre-exist in their underlying causes): milk turns into yoghurt. Milk is the underlying cause or substrate (*upadana-karana*) and yoghurt emerges as a product (*karya*) from it. *Satkaryavada* is a theory of causal process, accepted by the *Samkhya* and *Vedanta* traditions, according to which the effect pre-exists in a potential state in its underlying cause before its actualisation as an entity that is identified by its own name and form. Another example is clay as the underlying cause containing the pot. Here the causal process involves a modification (*parinama*) of a stable underlying reality and not the generation of a totally novel product. There is a strong link between the emergent effect and its causal substrate.

The effect is not produced as a reality distinct from its underlying cause. It is a specific rearrangement of that causal substrate.

The *satkarya* theory holds that *satta* (the supreme universal 'being-ness' or 'being-in-general') includes both the potential and the actual. So it is not the case that only the concrete and observable is real. Entities exist in either a subtle (unobservable) causal state (potentiality) or in actuality when they are called effects or products. The domain of potentiality is called *pradhana* and or *prakriti*.

See *Asatkaryavada*

Further reading: Bartley 2002; Halbfass 1992; Lipner 1986

Sautrantika: Buddhist school upholding a radical version of the view that objective reality is a flux of instantaneous points completely void of common features (*Kshanikatva*). They reject the view of the *Vaibhashikas* that we directly perceive physical objects consisting of real basic ingredients possessing essential natures and existing in past, present and future (*dharma*). They think that reality consists of unique momentary particulars (*svalakshana*) with a specific causal power. The existence of a particular is identical with the discharge of its causal power. Particulars cause sensory impressions of which the mind forms images. That there is an objective reality external to consciousness is inferred (*bahyartha-anumeyavada*) as the cause of those ideas that are independent of the will. They argue against *Vijnanavada* idealism that since the consciousness that is common to all cases of awareness is uniform while the representative contents (*akara*) of thoughts are different, the variety of experience must have extra-mental causes although we are not directly acquainted with them. The direct objects of awareness are not physical objects but ideas having their own forms. If blue is experienced, how can it be external? If it is not perceived, how can it be called external? We have an innate tendency to treat our concepts as copying reality as it is in itself. But the objects and causes of perceptual sensations are fleeting combinations of *svalakshana*s, awareness of which is filtered through mental images that are in some way coordinated with them. So there is no match between cause and representative content. Our experience of a rainbow is totally different from what causes it (*see*: *alambana*). *Sautrantikas* object to the *Vaibhashika* tenet that physical objects are built up out of partless atoms, that since the atoms have no parts (they would need boundaries if joined to others) they cannot combine to form larger whole things. Also, if the atoms are only manifested in this world for a very short time, it seems that by the time we perceive them they have gone.

See *Dharmakirti*

Further reading: Matilal 1986; Mookerjee 1975

Savikalpaka-pratyaksha (concept-laden perception): Buddhists following *Dignaga* and *Dharmakirti* radically divorce sensory perception from the process of conceptualisation in which the mind not only organises but also adds to what has been given in perception. In response to this, realist philosophers insist that there are two varieties of perception: non-conceptual and non-linguistic sensory perception (*nirvikalpa-pratyaksha*) and perception that involves concepts (*savikalpaka-pratyaksha)*. In the second variety, concepts identify and structure the information received from perceptual sensation. Sensory impressions are themselves true to reality. Conceptual perception discriminates the object as an individual instance of a kind and discerns its various properties. The key point is that it operates on what has been given: the mind discovers, it does not invent features or impose anything on reality. Some *Advaita-Vedantins*, following *Mandana Mishra*, held that preconceptual perception reveals undifferentiated pure being. This stimulated the reaction that the primary perceptual stage receives unconceptualised information about the shared and specific features of its objects. What is distinctive about *savikalpaka-pratyaksha* is that it brings the object into sharper focus and compares it with other objects belonging to the same kind.

Further reading: Bartley 2002; Matilal 1986

Shabda-bodha: understanding from words and sentences. A person understands what is said when they hear or read a grammatically correct sentence (*vakya*) expressing a genuinely possible state of affairs. Sometimes the speaker's intention (*tatparya*) is taken into account.
Further reading: Ganeri 1999

Shabda-pramana: language as an instrument of knowledge. It may inform or move to action. *Shabda* (lit. the sound of a word) may be the testimony of reliable persons or *Vedic* scriptural language (*shruti*), or the *Agamas* recognised as authorities by the non-*Vedic* or *Tantric* religious cults. Language is accepted as an instrument of knowledge in its own right by all philosophical schools excepting materialists, Buddhists and **Vaisheshikas**. The *Nyaya* school says that a person is a reliable authority when they are not in error, have no intention to deceive, are neither drunk nor confused and when their sense faculties are working normally.

The mainstream orthodox Ritualists (**Purva-Mimamsa**) and **Vedantins** hold that the relation between a Sanskrit word in the **Vedas** and the object that it means is innate, natural and eternal. According to both schools, the *Vedic* scriptures have no author, human or divine. They are simply given. *Vedic* language is only a source of knowledge about whatever lies beyond the range of sensory perception: thus it cannot be contradicted by those *pramanas* whose operation is restricted to the sphere of sense-based experience and nor can it contradict them.

The permanent relation obtains between general terms for kinds of things and particular entities. Thus, 'cow' in isolation stands for the generic property or form (*akriti*) shared by all individual cows. So the word–object connection is neither created when a calf is born nor broken when a cow dies. (Words refer to individuals in the context of a sentence.) Proper names are treated like general terms: *Indra* stands for the class of beings possessed of the powers defining the nature of that deity.) Ritualists think that authority is restricted to statements commanding actions and telling us how to perform them. *Vedantins* say that fact-asserting statements in the *Vedas* about God, the soul and its destiny are also authoritative. The *Nyaya* school thinks that the *Vedic* scriptures are an instrument of knowledge because God is their reliable author. The existence of God is established not from scripture but by inference.

Buddhists deny that there is an innate relation between word and object. They also deny that words have a power to express their objects automatically. If they had, people would not need to learn languages. They dismiss the intrinsic reliability of testimony since we can never know whether another person is being honest just by listening. Since linguistic understand involves some thought process, they include it under inference.

Further reading: Bartley 2002; Bilimoria 1988; Ganeri 1999; Lipner 1986

Shaiva Siddhanta (Kashmiri): *Tantric* ritual cult teaching that the God *Shiva* (*pati*), individual souls (*pashu*) and matter are really distinct. It bases itself on a collection of twenty-eight scriptures called *Tantras* or *Agamas*, which are believed to be the word of God. It flourished in Kashmir from the eighth to the eleventh centuries CE. A radically modified descendent survives to this day in south India as a devotional (*bhakti*) religion. Its most important thinker was *Ramakantha Bhatta* (950–1000 CE). Whereas monistic schools such as the *Trika* emphasised intuitive knowledge (*jnana*) as the way to liberation from rebirth, the *Siddhantins* insisted on the necessity of the performance of ritual action, subsequent to initiation (*diksha*) into the cult thanks to God's grace (*anugraha*). Following the ritual path just for its own sake will not generate **karma**. More crucially, it helps to remove an innate defect (*mala*) that has radically restricted the souls' potentially infinite innate powers of knowledge and action. *Mala* is ultimately responsible for subjection to **karma** and rebirth. Salvation, granted by *Shiva* when he judges the soul ready for it, is understood as becoming all powerful and all knowing, like the godhead.

Shiva is conceived as a deity with an interest in the world that is compassionately disposed towards **mala**-stricken human beings. He is said to possess an unlimited power (*shakti* – which may be represented as his female partner) comprising knowledge and action. He is all pervasive, not a being among beings. He is differentiated from the liberated souls by the fact that he is never subject to finite conditions.

Mala is a material substance (*dravya*) and needs an action to remove it. Knowledge of its presence is not enough. Whereas the *Tantric* votaries of the ferocious deities *Bhairava* and *Kali* believe that sectarian initiation annuls one's former caste, *Shaiva Siddhantin* initiation leaves **caste**, understood as an intrinsic physical property, intact. The initiate is thus able to fulfil his orthodox Brahminical social and ritual duties. His life of ritual duty, combining both orthodox and *Tantric* commitments, is consistent with mainstream orthodox Brahminical duty and caste purity (*varna-ashrama-dharma*).

The eternally real material cause of the physical universe is called **maya**. *Shiva* operates on this to create environments so that souls, embodied with limited powers of knowledge and action, may be freed from their **karma** by experiencing its fruits. *Shaiva Siddhantins* believe that creation and the organisation of spheres of experience is in harmony with the accumulated *karma* of individuals. When *Shiva* decides that a soul's *mala* has matured, he will move him to seek initiation, which induces the destruction of *mala*. The soul will be released at death, when the effects of its past *karma* have been exhausted.

Further reading: Cowell and Gough 1996; Filliozat 1994; Goodall 1998; Goudriaan 1992; Sanderson 1992

Shakti: power, especially that of a masculine god when personified as his female partner. Thus the goddess *Lakshmi* is the *Shakti* of *Vishnu*.

Shankara (c. 700 CE): renouncer and major theorist of non-dualistic *Advaita Vedanta*. He wrote commentaries on the *Brahma-sutras* that summarise the ideas of the major *Upanishads*, and the *Bhagavad Gita*. The *Upadesasahashri* ('Thousand Teachings') is also an important work.

Like all *Vedantins*, he held that transpersonal scripture (*shruti*) is the only means of knowledge (*pramana*) about whatever lies beyond the empirical world. And it is as an interpreter demonstrating the conformity of his beliefs with the *Upanishadic* texts that he may best be understood.

He thinks that the Absolute Reality (*Brahman*) is undifferentiated, relationless, static, contentless consciousness and bliss. It is beyond all oppositions such as that of knower and known. But due to primal ignorance (*avidya*) it somehow becomes the substratum of diversity. The self-evident conscious soul (*atman*), which is the constant witness (*sakshin*) of all mental states, is identical with *Brahman*.

Differentiation and action, albeit experienced, are ultimately unreal. All plurality of selves, mental events, objects, causes and effects is a function of beginningless ignorance generating the misapprehension of the self as a personalised agent and experiencer subject to *Vedic* social and ritual duties (*varna-ashrama-dharma*) and transmigration (*samsara*). The human person is a composite of spirit (*atman*) and matter. Such a composite has experiences and is subject to the illusion that it is an agent. This denial that the self is really an agent is crucial to *Advaita Vedanta*. Aversion to worldly life, and renunciation (*samnyasa*) of all ritual and *caste* duty precedes direct insight (*jnana-marga*) into the identity of the soul and *Brahman*. That intuition negates *avidya* and alone leads to release (*moksha*) from the series of births. Insight into the *Brahman-atman* state only arises from the accredited scriptures (*shruti*), which are the only means of knowledge about supernatural realities. Liberating insight is expressed in *Upanishadic* major statements such as 'That thou art' (*Tat tvam asi*), asserting the identity of the self and the Absolute.

Ritual action (*karman*) and devotion (*bhakti*), while purifying the mind, cannot of themselves produce release since they presuppose that differences are real and thus belong in the sphere of ignorance. In short, any form of action binds one to *samsara*.

The human life of the enlightened and liberated individual (*jivanmukta*) continues until what is termed the *karma* appropriate to the final existence has been exhausted. No fresh *karma* is generated after the renunciation of all ritually and ethically significant actions.

See *Neti Neti*, *adhyasa*

Further reading: Bartley 2002; Halbfass 1995; Mayeda 1979; Potter 1981; Ram-Prasad 2002; Thibaut 1904b

Shantarakshita (c. 700–50 CE): Buddhist philosopher whose *Tattvasamgraha* is an elaborate defence of the logical and epistemological theories of idealist *Vijnanavada*. This comprehensive work, with its commentary by

Kamalashila, is a valuable encyclopaedia of philosophical debates between realist and anti-realist schools.
  Further reading: Jha 1987; Matilal 1986; Siderits 1991

Sharira-shariri-bhava (soul–body model): this is *Ramanuja*'s
original idea that the Supreme Self is related to the individual selves (*jiva*), in a manner comparable to that in
which they are related to their material bodies. He defines
a body as an essentially dependent entity whose reason
for being consists in serving the purposes of a self that
controls it. Body depends upon soul in the fundamental
sense that it would not be an entity in the absence of a
soul. Soul and body are really distinct. Individual selves
and material things constitute the body of God in that
they are dependent upon God and exist to express his
glory. Just as the essential distinction between the individual selves and their bodies means that they are not
really affected by physical defects, so the difference between God and his body, the world, exempts him from
limitations. A physical body is an entity only if there is a
soul associated with it. As such it is a mode (*prakara*) of
a soul. *Ramanuja* maintains that the reference of words
for essentially dependent modes extends to whatever possesses the mode. Thus an embodied soul can be referred to
by expressions for its body, as when someone says, 'He is
the smiling, bald man over there'. Since every entity con-
stitutes the body of God, God can be directly signified by
all words. So all scriptural statements can be referred to
as ultimately referring to God in their literal senses.
  Further reading: Bartley 2002; Carman 1974; Lipner
1986

Sheshavat: the inference of a cause from an effect, as when
we infer the prior occurrence of sexual intercourse from
pregnancy.

Shri Harsha (1125–80): Indian exponent of the method of destructive argument (*vitanda*) who attempted in his *Khandanakhandakhadya* to establish the *Advaita-Vedantin* belief that the only genuine reality is undifferentiated reflexive and self-established awareness. He argues that both our reliable means of knowledge and the categories to which the realist ascribes objective existence are in fact indefinable and just matters of human convention. His method is to examine the definitions proposed by his opponents and to demonstrate that they involve inconsistencies. The only certainty is that self-aware (*svayam prakasha*) consciousness alone exists.

His negative criticisms of the definitions proposed by **Nyaya-Vaisheshika** thinkers prompted the often highly technical and sophisticated reformulations developed by the **Navya-Nyaya** school.

Further reading: Ganeri 2001a; Granoff 1978; Phillips 1996; Ram-Prasad 2002

Shruti (what has been heard): the **Vedas** and **Upanishads** are believed by mainstream orthodox Hindus to be authorless (*apaurusheya*), eternal and infallible when they refer to anything supernatural. The relation between the sound of a scriptural word and its object is innate, sounds participating in the natures of their referents. *Shruti* is held to be the only reliable means of knowledge (*pramana*) about the supernatural that is beyond sensory perception (*pratyaksha*) and inference (*anumana*).

Vedanta is the systematic interpretation of *shruti* statements about God, the soul and the origination of the cosmos.

There is also a body of literature known as *smriti* ('what has been remembered', that is, traditional) whose function is to clarify and support *shruti*. These works, which include the *Mahabharata*, **Bhagavad Gita** and some *Puranas*, are not *pramanas* because they do not bear directly on something that would otherwise be unknown.

Further reading: Halbfass 1991

Shunya (emptiness): *Nagarjuna* draws out the philosophical implications of the idea frequently expressed in the early *Mahayana* Buddhist 'Perfection of Wisdom' (*Prajnaparamita*) literature that everything is empty. He interprets this as meaning that nothing whatsoever has an essential, unchanging nature (*svabhava*) because the very notion is an impossible one. There are no real essences because essence means immutable nature and something with an immutable nature cannot participate in a process of change. That there are no essences extends to the basic mental and material atomic factors (*dharma*) that the *Abhidharma* Buddhists hypothesized as the ultimately real building blocks of the cosmos. *Dharmas* + *svabhava* = static reality. 'Emptiness' does not mean the same as 'interdependent origination' (*pratitya-samutpada*) because the basic atomic factors are not dependently originated, conditioned (*samskrita*) realities. To say that the *dharmas* lack essence is to reject the realist's requirement that there are ultimate facts that are mind-independent, that is, not conceptually constructed. To say that all things are empty of essential nature is to say that there are no classes or types of entities. In short, there are no real entities.

Nothing can be self-created or self-existent; nothing is entirely self-sufficient and independent of other things. The notion of immutable timeless essences makes no sense. Moreover, anything that arises in dependence of cause and conditions is also devoid of essential nature and is conceptually constructed.

The mere fact of its being caused does not entail that something lacks essence. What is incompatible with the existence of essences is the view that causal relations are forms of conceptual construction and not objective realities. We formulate in the categories of cause and effect what seem to us regular associations. But this is a projection that suits human interests. Insight into emptiness is the realisation that there is no absolute conception of reality that is accessible to us. It is a mistake to draw a distinction between what is ultimately real and what is only conceptually real, and between absolute truth and conventional truth. The truth is that there is no ultimate reality. There is no difference between *nirvana* and *samsara*.

Acceptance that there are no essences removes our need to invent and cling to ultimate truths, dogmatically held: an activity that reinforces our self-love.

Further reading: K. Bhattacharya 1998; Burton 1999; Garfield 1995; Lindtner 1982; Williams 1989

Skandhas: according to Buddhism the five components of personality, apart from which there is no further factor called Soul (*atman*). The components are: matter, sensation, habits, dispositions, thoughts and perceptions. They are always in a flux and human lives are processes belonging to a wider field of energies.

The five psychophysical components of personality are described as follows:

1. Form or corporeality (*rupa*): comprised of the four base elements, earth, water, fire and air and their derivatives which include the physical sense organs and their external objects.
2. Sensation or feeling (*vedana*): this may be physical or mental and is derived from contact between the six internal sense organs (five plus mind (*manas*) which relates to mental phenomena or thinkables (*dharma*))

and six types of sense data deriving from external objects.

3. Sense-perception (*samjna*): determinate perception involving recognition and naming and relating to the external objects.
4. Dispositions of character (*samskara*): accumulated **karma** and the volitions and intentions that derive from and are produced by it.
5. Thoughts (*vijnana*) grasp the characteristics of the six types of objects. It is of six kinds; visual, auditory, olfactory, gustatory, tactile and mental.

See *anatta*
Further reading: Collins 1982

Smriti see *Shruti*

Somananda (900–50 CE): original theorist of the **Pratyabhijna** school of Kashmiri *Shaivism*. His *Shivadrishti* expounds a form of absolute idealist philosophy that denies the reality of the physical independent of universal consciousness. The argument is that if there were a real difference in nature between consciousness and material objects, knowledge of the world would be impossible. Material things, whether atoms or concrete wholes, and consciousness are utterly different categories and cannot be related. Relation is possible only when categories have something in common. A relation between thinking minds and objects is possible if consciousness is the common factor present in everything. To be is to be a manifestation of consciousness. It follows that all conscious subjects are essentially the same. The universal consciousness is identified as the supreme godhead *Shiva* who is present everywhere. Everything is a manifestation of the single, divine consciousness. There are no real individual identities. Everything participates in the nature of everything else.

Human problems start when we just think of ourselves as isolated individuals with social identities confronting a separate material environment. The point of religious practice is the recovery of one's true identity as *Shiva* through the expansion of one's conscious energy. Somananda criticises *Advaita Vedantins* who think that the differentiated cosmos is an illusory manifestation (*vivarta*) brought about by mysterious ignorance, of the static, featureless Supreme Reality (*Brahman*). He attacks the idealism of the Buddhist *Vijnanavada* that admits streams of consciousness but regards our experience of the material world as merely subjective imagination. Moreover, Buddhists cannot allow that there is a stable subject doing the imagining. Commonsense realists are criticised for admitting individual centres of consciousness and agency, but distinguishing them from their physical environments in such a way that no sense can be made of their relation to it. *Shaiva Siddhantins* are castigated for positing themselves as individuals independent of godhead.

Further reading: Sanderson 1990; Torella 2002

Spanda: Kashmiri theological articulation of the view that god is ultimately to be understood as single, creative consciousness. This outlook becomes one of the components of *Abhinavagupta*'s syncretistic *Trika*. The 'Verses on Oscillation' (*Spanda Karika*) are alternatively considered to have been composed been composed by *Vasugupta* (850–900 CE) or by his pupil *Kallata*. They are the subject of a commentary (*Spanda Nirnaya*) by the *Trika* theorist *Kshemaraja* (1000–50 CE). There is also a commentary (*Spanda Pradipika*) from the point of view of a *Vishnu* cult by *Utpala Vaishnava* (925–75 CE). The

Spanda-Karikas teach that the god *Shiva* manifests itself as the cosmos. *Shiva* names a single, all-inclusive trans-individual self-aware consciousness spontaneously flashing forth as all subjects, acts and objects of awareness through its dynamic power of vibration (*spanda*). A limiting condition called *anava mala* reduces universal consciousness to limited subjects of experience embodied in particular circumstances (*mayiya-mala*) where they acquire a burden of good and bad **karma** which propels them into further spheres of experience.

Liberation (**moksha**) on the part of the fully enlightened person is understood as the realisation of one's identity as the creative principle that is the essence of all experiences.

Further reading: Dyczkowski 1987; Singh 1980

Sphota ('undivided meaning'): the grammarian and philosopher **Bhartrihari** saw that the primary linguistic fact is the sentence with an undivided meaning (*sphota*) and that individual words are abstractions from sentences. Meaning is not to be identified with evanescent sounds. Just as we do not understand a word after hearing its final element and combining it with remembered sounds of the preceding elements (when I hear 'mystery', I don't first think of mist), so we do not gradually understand a series of individual words and then combine them to understand the sentence. Rather, the latter is grasped immediately and instantaneously as a whole (*pratibha*: 'flash of insight') and not as the result of a mental synthesis. The meaning-bearer is not identical with the collection of sounds but is revealed by it. The word is as an entire meaningful symbol (*sphota*). It is a mental entity manifested by physical sounds. The unchanging word that conveys meaning is called *sphota*. It is distinct from the phonemes and is manifested by them. In normal language, it is the sentence, or rather contextual sequence of sentences, that is the bearer of meaning – that which is understood.

Phonemes in a single word and the individual words themselves are fictions that help grammarians to analyse and discuss language. Individual words are abstractions from sentences. We do not normally use them on their own. (Saying 'yes' or 'no' is a response to a sentence. 'Fire' means 'run for safety'.) Once it is accepted that it is the sentence rather than individual words that is primarily meaningful, it is a short step to the idea that it is the paragraph or chapter or whole text that is the bearer of significance. These larger contexts are themselves understood in the context of the whole of language. So it turns out that meaning is total and undivided: distribution into books, paragraphs, sentences and words are all cases of apparent fragmentation that serves human purposes. This holistic concept of meaning is then identified as the Absolute Reality. Wider contexts, sentences, words and letters can be seen as progressive fragmentary emanations of a semantic absolute in which thought and language are not differentiated prior to the emergence of words.

Further reading: Brough 1996a and 1996b; Matilal 1986 and 1990; Shastri 1959

Svabhava (literally 'own-being'): the essential nature shared by members of a kind of entities. It is understood as entirely self-sufficient and invariant. *Svarupa* ('own-form') usually means the same.

Svabhava-hetu: a form of inference developed by the Buddhist *Dharmakirti* in which the logical reason (*hetu*) shares the nature of the property to be proved (*sadhya*) or the *sadhya* shares the nature of the *hetu*. So we can reason that if something is an oak, it is a tree.

Further reading: Kajiyama 1998; Prasad 2002

Svabhava-pratibandha (natural regularity): the key feature of a valid logical inference (*prayoga*) is the invariant association (*vyapti*) between the logical reason (*hetu*) and what is to be established (*sadhya*). According to the Buddhist *Dharmakirti*, the invariant association (which he also calls 'inseparable linkage' or *avinabhava*) must be guaranteed by some sort of natural regularity. Only thus can we be sure that a universal proposition of the form 'All As are Bs' is true.

His theory of natural regularity attempts to underpin some forms of inseparable connection in the absence of objective universals (*samanya-lakshana*). He holds that we know that the connection between the logical reason and the property to be proved could not be otherwise (*niyama*) when the connection is either that between cause and effect (*tad-utpatti/karya-hetu* – 'fire and smoke') or a case of shared nature (*tadatmya/svabhava-hetu* – 'tree and oak'). This necessary relation is what he calls the natural regularity or *svabhava-pratibandha*. So we may infer from the fact of something's being an oak that it is a tree and from the presence of smoke to the presence of fire. This principle is applied in characteristically Buddhist arguments such as, 'If something is produced, it is perishable by nature'.

Dharmakirti's point is that the invariable association must be more than the product of a finite range of observed instances (*bhuyo-darshana*) as well as the lack of counter-examples (*adarshana-matra*), since that would leave open the possibility of our discovering exceptions in the future.

Dharmakirti thinks that while immediate sensory impressions relate directly to reality that consists of unique instantaneous particulars (*svalakshana*), the mental images and concepts that are formed about them do so indirectly. But *Dharmakirti* does not think that all our concepts are imaginary inventions. The instantaneous actualities behave in such a way that we can organise them under unifying concepts. Although the regularity (*svabhava-pratibandha*) between smoke and fire or that between something's being an oak and its being a tree holds primarily between two concepts, it also reflects a real state of affairs that causes us to make the connection between the concepts. **Dharmakirti** says that inference does not grasp the realities directly in that it operates by determining the object in a mental representation that is not itself the object. But because the representation of the object is understood because of some particular reality, the particular that is understood falls within the scope of the operation of inference.

Further reading: Dunne 2004; Tillemans 1999

Svabhava-vada (philosophical naturalism): the theory that the cosmos is unproduced and self-perpetuating. The cosmos is sustained by the mechanical operations of basic substances and their essential properties, regulated by natural laws.

See **Carvaka**

Svalakshana (unique instant): according to the Buddhist **Dignaga** and his school, objective reality (*paramartha-sat*) consists of momentary unique particulars, each with a specific causal efficacy. They take the Buddhist **Abhidharma** notion of the basic atomic mental and material factors (*dharma*) underlying everything, each having a type of essence or unchanging nature (*svabhava*), and subtract the *svabhava*. The remainder equals unique, inexpressible instants.

Each lasts just long enough for it to be replicated. Its existence is identical with the discharge of its causal activity. To be is to be effective. The *svalakshana* is a unique reality determined by a space, time and form that are specific to it. There are no objective general features: neither universals nor recurrent properties nor even resemblances. Unique particulars are the primary data of sensory perception, which is always non-conceptual and non-linguistic. The particulars are organised by automatic causal factors so that they occur in patterns such that produce mental images about which we construct concepts (*vikalpa*) that contribute to successful activity. Although there is a gap between the ways our minds work and the way things are we can still frame mental representations that help us to find our way around. *Samanya-lakshana* means the results of the process of mental construction by which we organise the real particulars that are the raw data of experience under general concepts that may be expressed in words. But we are mistaken if we suppose that our concepts copy reality as it is in itself.

Further reading: Hattori 1968; Kajiyama 1998; Matilal 1986; Mookerjee 1975; Torella 2002

Svartha-anumana see *Parartha-anumana*

Svasamvedana (intrinsic reflexivity of awareness): this is the view that all cognitions and feelings are directly aware of themselves or reveal themselves to the subject. If cognition were not perceived, perception of objects would not be possible. (That feelings are reflexively known is uncontroversial: there are no unfelt pains.) Every cognition is by nature aware of itself and does need to be the object of another cognition. The idealist version states that thoughts are *only* aware of themselves.

The *Nyaya-Vaisheshikas* reject this outlook: they think that most psychological episodes pass unnoticed. That is to say, I am currently receiving all sorts of information about the environment, but only some of that data is explicitly present to my consciousness. Pleasures and pains are not types of awareness, but they may become the objects of awareness. They do distinguish between the causal conditions giving rise to an experience and the subjective awareness of experience or what one feels. The dentist may be drilling a tooth, and touching the nerve, so all the conditions for pain are present. But happily my gum has been anaesthetised. Buddhists, who think that the notion of unfelt pains is nonsense, would argue that the anaesthetic blocks the efficacy of the physical causes that are necessary but not sufficient conditions for the experience of pain.

'Self-awareness' sometimes means that we are not just aware of what we experience, but also of the self as the subject of experience. The self is not known as the subject in the way in which external objects are known. The sense that one is the same self is simply given.

Further reading: Matilal 1986

Svatah Pramanya (the intrinsic veridicality or truthfulness of cognition): most Indian philosophers subscribe to some version of the thesis that a cognition is true, and thus a piece of knowledge, when its representative content corresponds to or pictures the extra-mental object. *Nyaya* philosophers and Buddhists deny that cognitions are true intrinsically and argue that an extra confirmatory factor (such as successful activity) is required (*paratah pramanya* – extrinsic veridicality of knowledge).

An undistorted perception of a novel sample of water does not count as a case of knowledge until it has been confirmed by some activity such as satisfying thirst. While success in practice is needed to reveal truth, this does not mean that truth is the same as successful activity. *Nyaya* adheres to the principle that nothing can exercise its proper function on itself. If a cognition cannot cognise itself, it cannot check its own validity, which stands in need of confirmation by another cognition.

The *Purva Mimamsaka* ritual tradition ritual insists that the *Vedic* scriptures are the only means of knowledge about social and religious duty (*dharma*). They hold that the authority of the *Vedas* is self-validating (*svatah pramanya*). The truth of the *Vedas* does not need confirmation or proof. *Purva Mimamsakas*, *Samkhyas* and *Vedantins* hold that cognitions are intrinsically valid in the sense that the very same conditions that generated the cognition also make it true. If cognitions are true intrinsically they do not need to be confirmed by successful activity (which would require another cognition, leading to an infinite regress). But, more strongly, the theory of intrinsic validity means that one can know something without knowing that one knows. Knowledge, having a true belief, does not require subjective certainty. A cognitive state with a reliable causal history (one generated by a means of knowledge – *pramana*) is knowledge immediately upon its occurrence and does not need the subject to check and justify it. A belief is automatically justified if there is an appropriate causal connection between its content and what it is about.

See *paratah pramanya*

Further reading: G. Bhattacharya 1989; K. Bhattacharya 1998; Burton 1999

Svatah siddha (self-evident proof): the view that the conscious self proves its own existence. It does not need to be established by anything other than itself. Knowledge of one's own consciousness is not mediated by an appropriate causal chain or by a reliable mechanism in the way in which our beliefs about external objects are. We have direct access to consciousness. There is something unique about our knowledge of our own experience.

Svayam prakasha (self-luminosity; reflexivity of consciousness): the view that when a subject cognises an object or fact simultaneously and in virtue of the same act he is aware of himself cognising that entity. For Buddhists such as **Vasubandhu**, **Dignaga** and **Dharmakirti** who deny that there is an enduring self that is the permanent background to experiences that it 'possesses', it is individual mental states that are characterised by self-awareness. For *Vedantins*, the permanent soul is self-aware.

More generally, some (**Vijnanavada** Buddhism, **Advaita-Vedanta**, **Ramanuja**, **Samkhya** and **Trika** Shaivism) appeal to the self-luminosity of consciousness as a way of expressing its foundational nature. Everything material needs the light of consciousness for its manifestation and determination as an existent entity. Consciousness requires nothing outside itself.

Further reading: Bartley 2002; Lipner 1986; Matilal 1986; Mohanty 1992

Tadatmya see *Svabhava-pratibandha*

Tantra: in parallel with Vedic orthodoxy, there is another broad family of religious traditions basing themselves on texts called *Tantras*, *Agamas* and *Samhitas*. Some of these cults are compatible with the Vedic tradition; others reject it. Their scriptures usually have four parts: metaphysical teachings (*vidya-pada*), ritual instructions (*kriya-pada*), ethical behaviour (*carya-pada*) and individual spiritual practice (*yoga-pada*). They describe the constitution of the cosmos, the nature of God, the soul in its original condition and as subject to bondage by *mala*, matter, and *karma*, ways to liberation, the acquisition of supernatural powers, temple-building, temple ceremonies, the creation of images of the deity, initiation rituals, and the use of mantras which are manifestations of divine power in the form of sounds. The *Agamas* have been graciously revealed by God as a path to salvation that is more easily understandable than the *Vedas*. They are superior to the *Vedas* since they have been spoken by God.

Further reading: Goodall 1998; Goudriaan 1992; Padoux 1990; Sanderson 1990

Tarka (suppositional reasoning): this is a pattern of reasoning applied when someone refuses to accept a conclusion. Its general form is to take the conclusion and imagine its contradictory, then show that the contradictory proposition leads to absurd or impossible consequences. So the originally disputed conclusion must be true. For example, we can infer the presence of fire on the mountain from the observation of smoke. But what if someone does not accept the principle (*vyapti*) that wherever there is smoke there is fire? If they deny that there is fire on the mountain, we say, 'If there is no fire on the mountain, then there is no smoke.' If the opponent denies this, we ask them to cite an instance of smoke without fire. This is impossible, so they have to accept, 'Where there is no fire, there is no smoke.' The opponent is assuming that there is no fire on the mountain. So their rationale must be: 'There is no smoke on the mountain, because there's no fire. Where there's no fire, there's no smoke. There's no smoke on the mountain.' But the conclusion is false because contradicted by observation. So the assumption that there is no fire on the mountain must be false and its contradictory true.

Tarka is not a reliable means of knowledge in its own right because it trades on conclusions whose truth has already been established.

Further reading: Ganeri 2001a

Tattva (type of reality; level of existence): metaphysical theories often include schemes of what they claim exists. The most influential is that of the *Samkhya* system, which holds that material nature (*prakriti*) is the source of the physical world. From it emerge: intellect (*buddhi*); the ego (*ahamkara*); the *manas*; the five sensory (*indriya*) and five motor faculties; the five subtle elements of sound, touch, visible form, taste and smell; and the five gross material elements (atmosphere, air, fire, earth and water).

Many traditions accept this framework, but some add supernatural levels of reality that accommodate other worlds or spheres of experience. The Kashmiri *Shaiva Siddhanta* cult places the *Shiva-tattva* at the pinnacle. It is followed by the *tattva* of divine power (*Shakti*), the *Sadashiva tattva*, the *Ishvara tattva* and the *Vidya-tattva*. These five are transcendental and contain pure worlds populated by released souls. Next come five *tattvas* applying particularly to souls: limited power of knowledge, limited power of action, passion, time and ethical consequentiality. At this point, the *Samkhya* scheme is introduced.

Trairupya-hetu (threefold logical reason): following *Dignaga*, Buddhist logicians say that, in a valid inference or proof, there must be an inseparable connection (*avinabhava-sambandha*) between the logical reason or proving property (*hetu*) and what is to be proved (*sadhya*). Wherever the reason occurs, there the *sadhya* occurs also. The satisfaction of three conditions guarantees this:

1. The logical reason must really be a property of the subject (*paksha*) of the inference.
2. The logical reason must be present in some instance (*sapaksha*) other than the subject of the inference, which is similar to that subject in that it too possesses the property that is to be proved.
3. Everything that lacks the property to be proved also lacks the proving property. There must be no instances where the proving property occurs and the property to be proved does not (*vipaksha*).

Take the inference that sounds (*paksha*) are impermanent (*sadhya*) because they are products (*hetu*). (Invariable association: whatever is produced is impermanent.) Here the *sapaksha* could be something uncontroversially impermanent such as a pot that also exhibits the property of being a product. It is open to us to cite an actual instance illustrating the joint absence of the property to be proved and the logical reason. The atmosphere would be a negative example because it both lacks impermanence and is not produced by effort.

Dharmakirti strengthens this basically inductive appeal to observed instances by insisting that the inseparable linkage that is pivotal in the inference must either be a case of causal necessitation (fire and smoke) or a matter of shared nature (if something is an oak, then it is a tree).

See *svabhava-pratibandha*
Further reading: Oetke 1994

Trika (*Shaiva* cult): a system of ritual originating and developing in Kashmir whose goal is the acquisition by the votary, who has undergone a *caste*-obliterating initiation ritual, of the supernatural powers of a triad (*trika*) of female deities, personifying the human-friendly as well as the terrifying and destructive aspects of existence. Associated with this cult was that of the eight mother goddesses and their expressions in families (*kula* – hence the term *Kaula* for forms of *Shiva* worship allied to the *Trika*) of female spirits called *Yoginis*. They may be invoked and pacified, in the impure cremation ground on the margins of society, with offerings of impure and hence potent substances such as blood, flesh, wine and sexual fluids. The cult adopted the horrific, all-devouring *Kalasamkarshini* form of the goddess *Kali* as the unifying form of the original three.

From 900 CE the *Trika* was in competition with the dualistic system of ritual and theology known as **Shaiva Siddhanta**, according to which really individual selves inhabit a physical world. Articulated in the sophisticated **Pratyabhijna** philosophy whose chief proponents are **Utpaladeva** and **Abhinavagupta**, the *Trika* was able to defeat the challenges posed by dualism, *Vedantic* illusionism and Buddhism. Its explicitly sexual rituals underwent a process of domestication and internalisation. This trend appears in the thought of **Abhinavagupta** where orgasm is understood as manifesting the expansion of blissful self-awareness, the same as the universal consciousness projecting all phenomena, annihilating one's self-centredness. Likewise, impure substances, which had been understood as sources of magical powers are held to induce ecstasy, a sense of freedom arising from violation of the taboo. *Trika* votaries understand bondage to worldly existence as the self-limitation that sees the orthodox values of purity and impurity as objective realities. Enlightenment is the realisation that anxious concern about *caste* and related values such as one's *Vedic* learning, family's status, prescribed conduct, conventional virtues and prosperity are aspects of an inauthentic identity.

Further reading: Sanderson 1990; White 2003

Udayana (1050–1100): realist philosopher who combined the *Nyaya* tradition of logic and epistemology with the *Vaisheshika* system of metaphysical categories and refuted a wide range of Buddhist theories. His major works include the *Atmatattvaviveka* in which he attacks many Buddhist doctrines. He rejects the view that everything is momentary as a prelude to establishing the reality of eternally enduring, omnipresent souls distinct from the body. He argues for the existence of a mind-independent world. He maintains that the possessor of properties is a reality actually and logically distinct from those properties (otherwise the soul would be inseparable from the stream of transitory experiences) and controverts the theory of the followers of *Nagarjuna* that everything is relative and empty (*shunya*) of own-nature (*svabhava*). Finally he refutes the anti-realist theory that what is not perceived by humans does not exist. The *Kiranavali* and the *Lakshanavali* belong to the *Vaisheshika* tradition of defining the fundamental categories of reality. The *Nyayavarttikatatparyaparishuddhi* is a contribution to logic and the theory of knowledge. The *Lakshanamala* synthesises *Nyaya* and *Vaisheshika* doctrines and techniques. The *Nyayakusumanjali* presents inferential proofs of the existence of God as an omniscient creator. The scriptures speak of God, but they are insufficient to prove his existence. We cannot say that God gives us the scriptures and then use those scriptures to prove the existence of God. Udayana formulates many arguments to demonstrate the existence of an all-knowing and all-powerful divinity who is the creator, preserver and destroyer of the repetitive cosmic process to which he is compassionately disposed.

Further reading: Chemparathy 1972; Potter 1977; Tachikawa 1981

Upadhi (imposed property): according to *Nyaya-Vaisheshika*, a classificatory property applied to a group of individuals. We can carve up reality in as many ways as we like, but only genuine universals (discovered, not invented) cut reality at the joints. Cowness is a natural kind, but cookness is a conventional classification summarising a range of skills and dispositions. A compound imposed property (*sakhandopadhi*) is a synthesis of two or more real classes. An example is beastness that combines hairy-ness, tailed-ness and four-legged-ness. It is artificial in that it cuts across natural kinds. *Devadattaness* (attributed to the unique individual *Devadatta*) is a simple imposed property (*akhandopadhi*).

In the realist **Bheda-abheda-vada** school of **Vedanta**, the term expresses accidental factors limiting the aspect of the Supreme Being from which the cosmos emerges.

Upalabdhi-lakshana-prapta: something in principle perceptible, although not currently present, to the senses. This hypothetical visibility is crucial to the theory that non-perception (*anupalabdhi*) can generate knowledge. 'There is no pot on the ground' ('the ground is qualified by pot-absence') is a piece of knowledge because we know that pots exist elsewhere and there could be one on the ground in front of us. But references to the absence of entities by nature imperceptible cannot be cases of knowledge. So, 'I do not see a ghost here' is not a means of knowledge for the absence of a ghost. Likewise, one cannot argue from the non-perception of other minds to their non-existence.

Upanishads: these works are included in the *Vedic* revelation, whose sounds the **Purva Mimamsaka** ritual theorists describe as authorless (*apaurusheya*) and eternal (**nitya**). Of the hundreds of works seeking to establish their authority by calling themselves *Upanishad*, there are thirteen composed probably in the seventh to the fourth centuries before Christ which are accepted as scriptural authorities by most traditions, especially **Vedanta**, claiming to represent mainstream orthodoxy. The most important texts are the *Brihad-Aranyaka, Chandogya, Taittiriya, Aitareya, Kaushitaki, Kena, Katha, Isha, Shvetashvatara, Mundaka, Prashna, Maitri* and *Mandukya*.

The four **Vedas** consist of hymns to and evocations of the *Vedic* gods. To these collections are attached texts called *Brahmanas* that comprise prescriptions for the performance of large-scale rituals by priests and their householder patrons. They also include explanations of the meanings of the ritual actions and words and explore correspondences between aspects of ritual and the cosmos. Typical statements are 'the sacrificial process represents time' and 'the sacrificial fire stands for the sun'. This style of explanation is extended in the *Upanishads* that were composed by people who had actually abandoned the performance of ritual. Their view is that the mental re-enactment of the meaning of the ritual is just as effective as its public performance. The *Vedic* deities come to be understood as personifications of aspects of human experience rather than objective realities.

The central themes of the *Upanishads* include:

Samsara: the negative evaluation of embodied human existence as belonging to a series of births confined to the physical conditions of space, time and causation. It is the sphere of mere becoming rather than true being, an endless cycle of repetitions through which one wanders aimlessly.

Karma: the notion that motivated and intentional ritual actions generate a latent potential that revisit agents in the shape future consequences and condemn them to repeated births.

Brahman (The Supreme Being): the idea that underlying the flux of empirical experience there is a static, all-pervasive, animating yet immutable reality that is immanent in the cosmos in that it is identical with the essence of everything including human beings.

Atman (soul): a changeless identity beyond space, time and finite human forms of experience. It is either identical with *Brahman* or intimately related to it. This centre of consciousness may become tied to a body, mind, will and senses. Burdened by the consequences of actions, this is what is reborn.

Release (*moksha*) from the series of births is possible through intuitive knowledge arising from the study of these texts.

Further reading: Hume 1949; Olivelle 1996; Radhakrishnan 1953; Rocher 1988

Utpaladeva (925–75 CE): following *Somananda*, a major theorist of the *Pratyabhijna* school of non-dualistic *Kashmiri Shaivism*. His principal protagonists are Buddhists belonging to the *Dignaga–Dharmakirti* tradition, whose representationalist theory of perceptual process he acutely translated into absolute idealism. *Dharmakirti* thinks that the mind forms images (*akara*) based on the sensory impressions that we have of objective reality consisting of a flux of unique momentary particulars (*svalakshana*). These mental images are then interpreted in concepts. *Utpaladeva* rejected the notion of a mind-independent realm of particulars. What the mind processes are manifestations (*abhasa*) that are themselves projected by the universal supreme consciousness. He thinks that our experience of a structured reality and our continuous awareness of ourselves as the same person requires that both subjects and objects belong to a single field of experience. Since experience (contra the Buddhists) requires a stable subject, there must be a single transcendental conscious substrate of the field of experience. While he denies that the *Nyaya* realism's dichotomy between a physical world that is real in its own right and individual subjects of experience is the whole truth, he integrates their categories (*padartha*) within a theory of absolute idealism according to which the cosmos is manifested by a single, transcendental conscious dynamism. Categories such as individual substance, action, relation, generic property, natural kinds, quality, space, time and the cause–effect relation are objective realities, not human conceptual constructions (*kalpana*) as the Buddhists hold, because they are manifestations (*abhasa*) projected by the transcendental consciousness. Manifestations are types. Individual entities are composed of many such universals.

Through its innate powers of unfettered will, infinite knowledge and action, the Absolute creates all subjects, objects and occasions of experience in a causally structured framework of space and time. The dynamic and utterly independent *Shiva*-consciousness is modelled on our experience of consciousness ever oscillating between the illumination of objectivity (*prakasha*) and reflective awareness (*vimarsha*). This is influenced by the grammarian *Bhartrihari*'s principle there can be no awareness without linguistic expression. *Utpaladeva* emphasises the liberty of individual subjective awareness, inspired by the compelling visions produced in meditation. Limited subjectivity is blamed on a principle called *mala*, which his dualist *Shaiva Siddhantin* religious competitors think is a substance in its own right. For him, it is just ignorance in these sense of a narrow-minded type of awareness.

Further reading: Torella 2002

Vacaspati Mishra (841 or 976 CE): a polymath whose works include the *Nyayavarttikatatparyatika* expounding *Uddyotakara*'s (600–50 CE) commentary on the aphorisms (*sutras*) basic to the *Nyaya* school; the *Tattvavaisharadi* on the *Yoga-Sutras*; the *Tattvakaumudi* on the *Samkhya-karikas*; the *Nyayakanika* on **Mandana Mishra**'s *Vidhiviveka*; the *Tattvabindu* (**Purva Mimamsa**) and the *Bhamati* commentary on **Shankara**'s commentary on the **Brahma-Sutras**. In the last, his definition of reality as undeniable self-evidence means that only the conscious inner self, the constant witness of all experiences, can be considered real. He claims that there are two forms of ignorance (*avidya*): a subjective psychological affliction (*klesha*), and the objective indescribable underlying cause of limited personality and what are experienced as the material objects. The limited self is the substrate (*ashraya*) of *avidya* and the absolute foundational reality (**Brahman**), understood as purely reflexive consciousness, its object. The content of the illusory experience of duality is due to cosmic *avidya*. The content of illusory experiences can neither be described as real nor as unreal; they persist for a time but are eventually negated by other experiences.

Further reading: Potter 1977; Ram-Prasad 2002

Vaibhashika: Buddhist school belonging to the *Sarvastivada* ('everything exists' family) holding that underlying all material and mental processes there are many types of real atomic factors (*dharma*). Each atomic factor and two modes of existence are actualised and non-actualised. Each occurs and disappears here in a single moment. Each has an essential nature (*svabhava*) that remains the same in past, present and future.

They claim that we are directly aware of objects made up of real physical atoms. Past and future *dharmas* exist if cognitions have real things as their objects. When there is an object, there arises a cognition. When there is no object, no cognition arises. If there were neither past nor future *dharmas*, there would be cognitions with unreal objects as their objective supports (*alambana*). But that is impossible. If there were no past or future *dharmas*, there would be no cognitions of past or future ones because of this lack of objective support. And if there were no past *dharmas*, how could there be future consequences of good or bad *karma*? How could there be the coming to fruition of past *karma* in the present?

Actualisation in the present moment is the exercise of a *dharma*'s effective activity (*karitram*). This efficacy is conditioned by and conditions other atomic factors. It means that a *dharma* is replaced by one of a similar kind. That the atoms pre-exist and continue to exist albeit in another dimension explains the continuities that we experience.

The most fertile source of information about this school is *Vasubandhu*'s *Abhidharmakoshabhashya*.

See *Abhidharma, Pratyaya*

Further reading: Potter 1996; Pruden 1988

Vaidharmya-drishtanta see *Hetu* and *Vipaksha*

Vaisheshika: one of the six orthodox Hindu philosophical outlooks (*darshanas*), this school is concerned with mapping the basic types of constituents and structures (*padartha*) of the universe. It was intimately associated with the *Nyaya* tradition, with which it eventually coalesced. The basic text is the *Vaisheshika-Sutra*, dating from about 100 CE, which is explained by *Prashastapada* (c. 500 CE) in the *Padarthadharmasamgraha*. *Vyomashiva*

(c. 800 CE) wrote the *Vyomavati* on *Prashastapada*'s work, and this was followed by Shridhara's *Nyayakandali* (991 CE). *Udayana* (c. 1050–1100 CE) produced the *Kiranavali* and *Lakshanavali* and effectively unified the *Vaisheshika* metaphysics with the *Nyaya* tradition of logical analysis and theory of knowledge.

The system is realistic in that the entities falling under the categories (*padarthas*) are held to be objective realities that we discover. They are all existent, knowable and nameable: if not by us, by God. Knowledge reveals a world independent of subjectivity. These realists minimise the creativity of consciousness that they treat as the passive recipient of data about ready-made realities external to it. This involves treating relations, qualities, universal properties and even absences as entities.

Understanding the categories (*padartha*) is held to lead to ultimate well-being.

Further reading: G. Bhattacharya 1989; Cowell and Gough 1996; Ganeri 2001a; Halbfass 1992; Potter 1977

Vasana: Buddhist view that traces of past experiences, deliberate choices and actions linger in a stream of experiences that we call a person. They form a 'mind-set', a stock of concepts, conditioning what one decides, does and undergoes.

Vastubalapravritta-anumana (inference tracking objective reality): Buddhists following **Dharmakirti** think that conceptual thought and language are at a distance from reality as it is in itself. This is because the objective sphere of unique momentary particulars (*svalakshana*) causes sensory impressions that are converted into mental images, which are in turn interpreted and structured in concepts by the constructive mind. An inference such as 'Sound is impermanent, because it is a product' is thoroughly conceptual. But it is not a purely subjective invention. The concepts it uses are indirectly related to objective reality that has been received in sense perception. So inferences involving them track objective reality.

See *Svabhava-pratibandha*

Vasubandhu: (c. 400 CE): Buddhist philosopher who moved from the *Sautrantika* representationalist school and became an idealist (*Vijnanavada*). He rejected the *Vaibhashika* Buddhist view that we are directly aware of objects made up of real physical atoms. An atom is partless and indivisible. But if atoms come together they will have sides. If they coalesce, there will be no increase in extent. If they have no dimension, they cannot combine to form larger objects. If they have dimension, they will be divisible. He also rejected the *Sautrantika* view that we can infer extra-mental reality as the cause of our perceptual sensations.

His view is that unenlightened people lead a life dominated by craving, aversions and delusions. Enlightened people who are detached from the objects of sense realise that the world is a fabric of appearances and are free from desires, aversions and delusions; in particular, the delusion that one is fundamentally an enduring, substantial soul, a 'further fact' over and above the stream of one's psycho-physical continuity. Awareness of a mind-independent physical world is the product of habitual construction by ideas projecting themselves as if external rather than of direct cognition of material reality. People are individualised not through relations to external circumstances but by a 'mindset' consisting of their inherited traits, attitudes, moods, emotions and memories. Deconstruction of these purely subjective factors encourages detachment from everyday experience.

He thinks that individual cognitions in a mental series (*samtana*) are aware of themselves. An awareness is simultaneously and in virtue of the same act self-cognised, just as a lamp illuminates itself while illuminating an object. This tenet of the reflexivity of consciousness is central to the idealist outlook: it shows that an idea can be the object of another idea and that there is no need to posit physical objects as the causes of our thoughts.

Vasubandhu wrote the *Abhidharmakosha Bhashya*, which is a critical survey from a *Sautrantika* point of view of Buddhist realist schools. Other works include: the *Karmasiddhiprakarana*, which is a *Sautrantika* critique of realist notions of how *karma* works and an attempt to reconcile atomistic impersonality with moral responsibility and consequentiality; the *Madhyantavibhagashastra* (idealist); the *Trisvabhavanirdesha* (idealist); the *Vimshatika* and the *Trimshika* (idealist).

Further reading: Anacker 1984; Matilal 1986; Pruden 1988; Ram-Prasad 2002; Stcherbatsky 1970; Wood 1991

Veda: the *Rig, Sama, Yajur* and *Atharva* Vedas are regarded by mainstream orthodox Hindus as an authorless (*aparusheya*), timeless and infallible repository of all knowledge. Their meanings are obscure and open to interpretation. The various orally transmitted Vedic traditions are held to be the only source of our knowledge about social and religious duty in accordance with the natural universal order (*dharma*). The *Purva Mimamsa* theorists of ritual say that *dharma* is that which is indicated by Vedic ritual prescriptions (*vidhi*).

The *Vedas* were held to have been received and promulgated by seven primordial 'seers' (*rishi*). The tradition was orally preserved by priestly Brahmin families maintaining particular traditions. The basic component of each of the four *Vedas* is its collection (*Samhita*) of verses (*mantra*),

evocative of the divinities in whose natures they participate, which are used in rituals. Attached to each *Samhita*
are texts called *Brahmanas* which prescribe, describe and
elucidate the purposes of the sacrificial rituals. They posit
correspondences between aspects of the rites and features
of the macrocosm, the social structure and the human
body. It was believed that ritual performance orders, sustains and perpetuates the universe, creating new time and
ensuring the regular succession of the seasons. There are
also the *Aranyakas* ('Forest Books') that speculate about
the 'inner' meaning of the rituals and are closely associated with the *Upanishads*.

Some *Rig Vedic* hymns contain speculations of a cos-
mological and metaphysical nature. *Rig Veda* 10.129 asks
what there was before existence (*sat*) and non-existence
(*asat*) prior to death and immortality, light and dark. The
hymn conveys a sense of genuine philosophical perplex-
ity and awe. Such inquiries will come to fruition in the
Upanishads.

Further reading: Flood 1996; Gonda 1975; O'Flaherty
1981

Vedanta (lit. 'end of the Veda' = the *Upanishads*): *Vedanta*
or *Uttara Mimamsa* is the systematic interpretation of the
Upanishads either by direct commentary upon them or
by explanation of the summaries of their contents in the
Brahma-Sutras. The *Bhagavad Gita* is also a key authority. Most *Vedantins* were worshippers of *Vishnu*. There
are three antagonistic schools: *Advaita* (Reality is non-
dual), *Vishishta-advaita* (Unity of Complex Reality) and
Dvaita (Dualism). They all agree that eternal scripture
(*shruti*) is the sole means of knowledge (*pramana*) for
what is beyond the scope of sensory perception and inference. *Vedantins* hold that it is the *Upanishads* (the
knowledge portion or *jnana-kanda* of the *Vedas*) that

provide information about the Supreme Being (*Brah-man*), the soul (*atman*) and the relation between the two, the origin of the universe from *Brahman*, retributive causality (*karma*), transmigration (*samsara*) and the means to and nature of ultimate liberation from rebirth (*moksha*). *Vedantins* seek a systematic interpretation of the *Upanishads*, believing that they have a unified overall meaning.

Whereas the theorists of ritual performance (*Purva-Mimamsakas*) were concerned with and insisted upon the primary meaningfulness of *Vedic* action-commands (*vidhi*) bearing on ritual actions, *Vedantins* focus upon the fact-asserting or descriptive texts (*arthavada*) referring to already existent entities or states of affairs, rather than 'things to be done' (*karya*). Both traditions developed sophisticated techniques of textual exegesis and argued about whether ritual performance is a path to salvation on its own in comparison with intuitive insight (*jnana*), devotion to God (*bhakti*) and divine grace (*prasada*).

All schools assume that effects do not differ essentially from their underlying or substrative causes. It follows that the cosmos is not essentially different from the Supreme Being that is its cause. *Madhva* is an exception here in that he thinks that God produces the cosmos out of eternally real prime matter that is distinct from him.

Further reading: Bartley 2002; Lipner 1986

Vijnanavada (*Yogacara*; *Cittamatra*): *Mahayana* Buddhist school denying that there are any physical objects. Our apparent experience of a physical world results from consciousness' appearing to itself in the form of ideas that we mistakenly interpret as standing for external objects. Having mentally constructed a world of objects, we imagine individual subjects perceiving it by acts of cognition. They claim that what is material cannot appear to consciousness: 'If blue is perceived, then how can it be called external? And if it is not perceived, how can it be called external?' Moreover, since blue and the awareness of blue always occur together, they are not different (*sahopalambha-niyama*).

If physical objects external to the mind existed, they would be either enduring whole entities or temporary configurations of atoms. The Buddhist *Vaibhashika* realists claimed that we directly perceive physical objects that are composed of atoms. An atom is partless and indivisible. But if atoms come together they will have sides (a type of part). If they coalesce, there will be no increase in extent. If they have no dimension, they cannot combine to form larger objects. If they have dimension, they will be divisible. Idealist Buddhists reject the notion of the integral whole (*avayavin*) over and above its parts because we do not cognise a single substance, itself consisting of no parts, apart from a collection of parts. If this is problematic, so much more so is that of categories such as universal property, the inherence relation, quality-particular, and substance which are applied to them by the *Nyaya-Vaisheshikas*.

Sautrantikas say that we cannot know momentary reality but only our representations of it, on the basis of which we infer the existence of mind-independent reality. The *Vijnanavadins* respond that we do not need to infer an objective reality as the casual basis of our experience, which is intelligible simply in terms of a beginningless stock of impressions left by previous ideas.

Awareness occurs in dreams and hallucinations without any external objects lending it causal support (*alambana*). It may be argued that the organised nature of waking awareness implies that we know objects at particular times and places. Moreover, much experience is shared by many and is not private. *Vasubandhu* responds that organisation may be dreamt and that there can be public delusions.

The variety of ideas is explained by the notion of a storehouse consciousness (*alaya-vijnana*).

Further reading: Anacker 1984; Matilal 1986; Ram-Prasad 2002; Wood 1991

Vikalpa (conceptual thought): for Buddhists following *Dignaga* and *Dharmakirti*, *vikalpa* means a concept that we construct out of the data of sensory awareness. Sense perception grasps unique particulars (*svalakshana*) lasting only for a moment. Only the unique particulars are real because they alone are causally effective. Cognitions involving apparently shared features of objects are conceptual interpretations based on experiences of particulars. Objective reality is strictly ineffable, since it includes no general features. It causes experiences, although their subjective content (*vishaya*) does not mirror it. But to find our way around successfully, we need to make discriminations using concepts and words. Some concepts, and elaborated conceptual schemes, apply more adequately than others to objective reality: that is, they work better for us in leading to successful activity. *Vikalpas* interpret and organise the data of perceptual experiences, making them intelligible and serviceable. This sort of conceptual construction differs from the free play of imagination, which is not in touch with objective reality. Conceptual construction depends upon the objective realm even if the ways in which our minds work do not accurately represent the way things are when left to themselves. Conceptualisation involves generalisations and there are no objective generalities. The store of human concepts, built up from impressions derived from a beginningless series of previous experiences, is transmitted down the generations via shared language. Language and conceptualisation always go together. As *Dignaga* says, 'Speech is born out of conceptual construction and conceptual construction is born out of speech.'

A problem arises when people overlook the purely conventional nature of what are only human ways of thinking and suppose that they correspond to objective realities. Error occurs when conceptual thought takes its own forms to correspond directly to reality. Since reality consists of momentary unique particulars, general concepts cannot represent it exactly. Still, a thought is reliable if it is causally related to the actual object.

See *Grahya-grahaka-vibhaga*

Vipaksha: in an inference, one of the guarantees of the invariable association of the logical reason with the property to be proved is that there are no instances where the logical reason (*hetu*) occurs and the property to be proved (*sadhya*) does not. If we want to establish the presence of fire on a mountain top and have seen smoke, we would appeal to the general principle that wherever there is smoke there is fire. The kitchen would be a positive example exemplifying the joint presence of the reason and the property to be proved. A lake would be a *vipaksha* in that it constantly exhibits the absence of fire and the absence of smoke. It is not necessary to cite a counter-positive example: what is crucial is that there is no knowledge of any case where the logical reason is found in the absence of the property to be proved.

Viruddha-hetu (contradictory logical reason): a type of fallacy (*hetvabhasa*) in which the logical reason (*hetu*) is defective because it never occurs where the property to be proved (*sadhya*) occurs: that is, it contradicts what one wants to prove. Examples: 'There is fire on the mountain, because it is icy'; 'Sound is eternal, because it is produced.'

An inferential argument for the existence of God might run, 'The world has an omniscient creator, because it is a complex product; like a pot.' Here, the pot example invites the accusation that the reason is contradictory because it leads to the conclusion that the world has a creator of finite intelligence.

Vishesha (ultimate particularity): according to *Vaisheshika*, these are unique features of the basic and simple eternal substances (*nitya-dravya*: atoms, atmosphere, time, space, souls (*atman*) and minds (*manas*)), distinguishing them from each other. Whereas complex entities are differentiated by the different arrangements of their parts, eternal substances are partless. So each must have its own individualising feature. They account for the unique and basic identities of these kinds of entity. The *vishesha* belonging to a soul, which is a non-conscious principle of continuity according to *Nyaya-Vaisheshika*, is what differentiates it from every other soul.

Vishishta-advaita (School of *Vedanta*): this is the sophisticated theological articulation of the devotional *Shri Vaishnava* cult, where the term *Vishishtadvaita* is interpreted as meaning 'non-duality' of a differentiated reality: that is to say, reality is a single, structured, ultimately intelligible totality that is internally complex.

The most prominent theorists of this tradition are *Yamuna*, *Ramanuja* and *Vedantadeshika*.

Vivarta-vada: *Advaita Vedanta* theory that the differentiated cosmos, including us as individual centres of awareness and agency, is only an illusory projection of the conscious foundational cause that is the sole reality.

Vyakti: an individual instance of a kind or universal property.

Vyapaka-vyapya see *Pervader-pervaded relation*

Vyapti (pervasion/invariable concomitance): technical concept in logic. A pervades B when it occurs in all or more of the instances where B occurs. Fire pervades smoke. Having an agent pervades being a created product. Impermanence pervades being a product. The factor of greater extent is called the pervader (*vyapaka*) and that of lesser extent the pervaded (*vyapya*). This means that A invariably accompanies B: smoke is always accompanied by fire and thus serves as a sign, logical reason and proving property (*hetu*) of the presence of fire. Knowledge of pervasion is the instrumental cause of a piece of knowledge arrived at by an inferential process (*anumana*). The generalisation 'Wherever there is smoke, there is fire' is a case of *vyapti* – smoke is the logical reason and fire is what is to be proved. The occurrence of the pervaded (smoke) implies the occurrence of the pervader (fire). The absence of the pervader implies the absence of the pervaded. Where there is smoke there is fire. Where there is no fire, there is no smoke. There is a range of views about the nature of the statement of pervasion: some think that it is a generalisation about many observed instances to which no counter-example has been found; others hold that once we have seen fire and smoke together our minds grasp the link between the universal properties smokiness and fieriness and we realise that smoke always occurs with fire (*samanya-lakshana*); later Buddhists think that the relation between pervader and pervaded is a natural regularity (*svabhava-pratibandha*) involving cause and effect (fire and smoke) or a shared nature (something's being a tree because it is an oak).

Further reading: G. Bhattacharya 1989; Ganeri 2001b; Oetke 1994; Prasad 2002

Vyavahara: everyday activity, thought and language. It is sometimes thought to conceal the true reality.

See *Advaita-Vedanta, Paramartha-sat*

Yamuna (966–1038 CE): South Indian Tamil *Shri Vaishnava* philosopher of the path of devotion to God (*bhakti-marga*). His works include the *Siddhitraya*, the *Agamapramanya* and the *Gitarthasamgraha* ('Summary of the Meaning of the *Bhagavad Gita*'). He was instrumental in the formulation of what came to be known as the *Vishishta-advaita Vedanta* theological philosophy developed by *Ramanuja*.

Yamuna thought in terms of three basic types of reality: God, individual conscious selves and matter. He argued for the existence of God on the grounds that the universe must be something produced since it consists of parts. The organisation of the parts and the occurrence of experiences in line with the accumulated merit and demerit of human beings mean that there must be an all-knowing and all-powerful maker. God is understood in personal terms, interacting with his devotees with whom he is intimately connected, although distinct from them.

Human beings are combinations of body and soul. Souls are disembodied individual subjects of thoughts and feelings. The soul is immediately known to be present (*svayam prakasha*) in all conscious experiences, whether or not they are of external objects. *Yamuna* understands consciousness as a permanent feature of the soul, which is the unchanging witness of its changing experiences.

In the *Gitarthasamgraha*, he claimed that the *Bhagavad Gita* urges us to love God (*bhakti-marga*), which is the way to gain release from the series of births. He understands the supreme goal as a sort of personal relationship with God in heaven.

Further reading: Bartley 2002; Buitenen 1953; Mesquita 1988; Neevel 1977

Yoga: a discipline aiming at salvation by purifying and perfecting the soul through the elimination of distracting thoughts and feelings. This involves both physical and mental self-control. The basic text of the classical Yoga school (*darshana*) is Patanjali's Yoga Sutra (c. 200 BCE–400 CE). The Yoga Sutra defines its subject as the restraint of all mental modifications – that is to say, the suppression of all forms of extroverted thought and feeling (*citta-vritti-nirodha*). Classical Yoga accepts the *Samkhya* dualism of primal matter (*prakriti*) and pristine conscious souls (*purusha*) but believes in the existence of God (*Ishvara*) who is a conscious individual unique in that it is never subject to *karma*. God initiates the world process by connecting conscious subjects with matter.

Souls, entangled in a morass of fluctuating mental and material phenomena, recover their true natures as pure consciousness when mentality (*buddhi*), ego (*ahamkara*) and the faculty coordinating the senses (*manas*) cease. To achieve this the mind–body complex with its passions, fleeting experiences, memories and expectations must be disciplined and focused upon a single point. Taxing asceticism (*tapas*), *mantra*-recitation, the study of scriptures about liberation (*svadhyaya*), and the direction of the mind to *Ishvara* all lead to contemplation (*samadhi-bhavana*) and the attenuation of the defects (*klesha*) of ignorance, egoism, desires, dislikes and obsessive attachments. Ignorance (*avidya*) – the perception of the impermanent as permanent, the impure as the pure, pain as pleasure and non-self as self – is the basic problem.

The eight stages of the physical, moral and mental discipline that form classical *Yoga* are:

Self-restraint (*Yama*): non-violence, honesty in thought, word and deed, sexual restraint and lack of greed.

Discipline (*Niyama*): interiorisation, tranquillity, asceticism, mantra recitation, the study of texts on liberation, and attention to God.

Physical postures (*Asana*): exercising control over the psychosomatic complex.

Breath-control (*Pranayama*): regulation and reduction of the processes of inhalation and exhalation that increase psychophysical control.

Withdrawal of the senses from their objects (*Pratyahara*) and direction of attention to the inner self.

Attention (*Dharana*): fixing the mind on a single point (that is, an object of meditation).

Meditation (*Dhyana*): the uninterrupted continuity of awareness about the object of meditation.

Profound contemplative introversion (*Samadhi*).

The state of liberation from rebirth is understood as one of wholeness and isolation (*kaivalya*) where consciousness experiences only itself. It occurs when the constituents of material nature (*gunas*) no longer operate in relation to the individual centre of consciousness. The soul recovers its true form, disjoined from mental modifications.

Further reading: Whicher 1998; Woods 1927

Yogacara see *Vijnanavada*

English–Sanskrit Glossary

Absence: *abhava*
Absolute Being: *Brahman*
Absolute Reality/Truth:
  paramartha-sat
Action: *karman; kriya*
Agreeing example: *sapaksha*
Atomic factor: *dharma*
Attribute: *visheshana; dharma*
Basic ingredient of reality:
  dharma
Caste: *varna; jati*
Category: *padartha*
Causal effectiveness: *arthakriya-*
  karitva
Causal efficacy: *arthakriya-*
  karitva
Class: *jati*
Class-property: *samanya*
Cognition: *jnana*
Cognitive authority: *pramanya*
Cognitive episode: *jnana*
Cognitive instrument: *pramana*
Concept: *vikalpa*
Concept-laden perception:
  savikalpaka-pratyaksha
Conceptual construction:
  kalpana
Conceptualisation: *kalpana;*
  vikalpa
Conditioned origination:
  pratitya-samutpada
Conjunction: *samyoga*

Constituents of personality:
  skandha
Conventional reality/truth:
  vyavaharika-satya; samvriti;
  prajnapti
Co-referentiality:
  samanadhikaranya
Definition: *lakshanam*
Dependent Origination: *pratitya-*
  samutpada
Desire: *iccha; raga*
Determinate perception:
  savikalpaka-pratyaksha
Devotion: *bhakti*
Disagreeing example: *vipaksha*
Dualism: *Dvaita*
Duty: *dharma*
Effects do not pre-exist in
  material cause: *asat-karya-*
  vada
Effects pre-exist in material
  cause: *sat-karya-vada*
Egoism: *ahamkara*
Emptiness: *shunyata*
Entity: *padartha; dravya; vastu;*
  bhava
Essence: *svabhava*
Essence less: *nih-svabhava*
Essential connection: *svabhava-*
  pratibandha
Essential nature: *svabhava*
Eternal: *nitya*

Example (of pervasion): *dristanta*
Exclusion: *apoha*
Extrinsic veridicality: *paratah pramanya*
Factor in an action or event: *karaka*
Feeling: *samvedana*
Frustration: *duhkha*
Generality: *samanya*
Generic form: *akriti*; *samsthana*
Generic property: *samanya*; *jati*
God: *Ishvara*
Grammatical co-ordination: *samanadhikaranya*
Ignorance: *avidya*
Ignorance as positive force: *bhava-rupa-avidya*
Illusion: *maya*
Illusory change: *vivarta*
Imagination: *kalpana*
Immediate experience: *anubhava*
Impermanent: *anitya*
Imposed property: *upadhi*
Indefinability: *anirvacaniya*
Indeterminate perception: *nirvikalpaka-pratyaksha*
Individual substance: *dravya*
Individuator: *vishesha*
Inference: *anumana*
Infinite regress: *anavastha*
Inherence: *samavaya*
Inherence cause: *samavayi-karana*
Inherent nature: *svabhava*
Injunction (ritual): *vidhi*; *niyoga*
Inner Sense: *manas*; *antah karana*
Inseparable connection: *avinabhava*
Instrument of knowledge: *pramana*
Instrumental Cause: *nimitta-karana*
Intellect: *buddhi*

Intrinsic reflexivity of consciousness: *sva-samvedana*; *sva-prakasha*
Intrinsic validity: *svatah pramanya*
Intrinsic veridicality: *svatah pramanya*
Intuitive insight: *jnana*
Invariable association: *vyapti*
Invariable concomitance: *vyapti*
Knowable entity: *prameya*
Knowledge: *prama*
Knownness: *jnatata*
Level of reality: *tattva*
Liberation from rebirth: *moksha*; *mukti*
Limiting adjunct: *upadhi*
Locus of properties: *dharmin*
Logical fallacy: *hetvabhasa* [*hetu-abhasa*]
Logical reason: *hetu*
Logical sign: *hetu*
Major term: *sadhya*
Manifestation (produced by or in consciousness): *abhasa*
Material cause: *upadana-karana*
Material nature: *prakriti*; *pradhana*
Meaning: *artha*
Memory traces: *Samskara*
Mental content: *vishaya*
Mental image: *akara*
Mental impressions: *vasana*
Mental modification: *citta-vritti*
Mental traces: *vasana*
Method of agreement and disagreement: *anvaya-vyatireka*
Metonymy: *lakshana*
Middle term: *hetu*
Mind: *manas*
Minor term: *paksha*
Misconception: *avidya*

Mode: *prakara*
Modification: *parinama*
Modifier: *prakara*
Momentariness: *kshanikatva*
Monism: *Advaita*
Natural connection: *svabhava-pratibandha*
Natural kind: *jati*
Natural law: *dharma*
Negative supporting example: *vipaksha*
Nescience: *avidya*
Non-cognition: *anupalabdhi*
Non-dualism: *Advaita*
Non-inherence cause: *asamavayi-karana*
Non-qualificative perception: *nirvikalpaka-pratyaksha*
Objective ground: *alambana*
Objective reality: *vastu*
Objective support: *alambana*
One's station and its duties: *sva-dharma*; *varna-ashrama-dharma*
Own nature: *svabhava*
Particular-quality: *guna*
Perception: *pratyaksha*
Perceptual sensation: *nirvikalpaka-pratyaksha*
Permanent: *nitya*
Personality disposition: *Samskara*
Pervasion: *vyapti*
Positive supporting example: *sapaksha*
Pre-conceptual perception: *nirvikalpaka-pratyaksha*
Presumption: *arthapatti*
Prime Matter: *prakriti*
Principle of identity: *atman*
Probandum: *sadhya*
Probans: *hetu*
Proper form: *svarupa*

Property: *dharma*; *visheshana*
Qualificand: *visheshya*
Qualificative perception: *savikalpaka-pratyaksha*
Qualifier: *visheshana*
Quality: *guna*
Quality-particular: *guna*
Rebirth: *samsara*
Reductio ad absurdum: *prasanga*
Reflexivity of consciousness: *svasamvedana*; *svayam prakasha*
Release from rebirth: *moksha*; *mukti*
Reliable means of knowledge: *pramana*
Renunciation: *samnyasa*
Rule of co-apprehension: *sahopalambha-niyama*
Scripture: *shruti*
Self: *atman*
Self-established: *svatah siddha*
Self-illuminating: *svayam-prakasha*
Self-revealing: *svayam-prakasha*
Sense faculty: *indriya*
Sense-organ: *indriya*
Separable connection or relation: *samyoga*
Series of experiences: *samtana*
Settled conclusion: *siddhanta*
Site of inference: *paksha*
Soul: *atman*
Soul–Body Model: *sharira-shariri-bhava*
Soulless: *anatta*; *nairatmya*
Stage of life: *ashrama*
Storehouse consciousness: *alaya-vijnana*
Strand (of material nature): *guna* of *prakriti*.
Stream of experiences: *samtana*
Subject of inference: *paksha*

Substance: *dravya*
Substrate (of properties): *dharmin*
Substrative cause: *upadana-karana*
Suffering: *duhkha*
Superimposition: *adhyasa*
Testimony: *shabda-pramana*
Theory: *vada*
Thing: *artha*
Threefold logical reason: *trairupya-hetu*
Transformation: *parinama*; *vikara*
Transmigration: *samsara*
Trope: *guna*

Type of reality: *tattva*
Underlying cause: *upadana-karana*
Undesirable entailment: *prasanga*
Unique differentiating feature: *vishesha*
Unique momentary particular: *svalakshana*
Universal property: *samanya*
Unwanted Consequence: *prasanga*
Warrant: *hetu*
Whole entity: *avayavin*
Will: *iccha*
World renunciation: *samnyasa*

Glossary of Headwords in Text with Diacritical Marks

Abhava: Abhāva
Abhihita-anvaya-vada:
  Abhihitānvayavāda
Abhranta: Abhrānta
Abhuta-parikalpa:
  Abhūtaparikalpa
Adarshana-matra:
  Adarśanamātra
Adhyasa: Adhyāsa
Adhyavasaya: Adhyavasāya
Advaita-Vedanta:
  Advaita-Vedānta
Ahamkara: Ahaṃkāra
Ahimsa: Ahiṃsā
Akasha: Ākāśa
Akriti: Ākṛti
Alambana: Ālambana
Alata-cakra: Alāta-cakra
Alaya-vijnana: Ālaya-vijñāna
Anaikantika-hetu:
  Anaikāntika-hetu
Anavastha: Anavasthā
Anekanta-vada: Anekānta-vāda
Anirvacaniya-khyati:
  Anirvacanīya-khyāti
Antarvyapti: Antarvyāpti
Anumana: Anumāna
Anuvyavasaya: Anuvyavasāya
Anvita-abhidhana:
  Anvita-abhidhāna

Anyatha-khyati: Anyathā-
  khyāti
Arthakriya: Arthakriyā
Arthapatti: Arthāpatti
Asatkaryavada: Asatkāryavāda
Ashrama: Āśrama
Atma-guna: Ātma-guṇa
Atman: Ātman
Avidya: Avidyā
Bhagavad Gita: Bhagavad Gītā
Bhartrihari: Bhartṛhari
Bhaskara: Bhāskara
Bhava-rupa-avidya:
  Bhāva-rūpa-avidyā
Bhava-vikara: Bhāva-vikāra
Brahma-sutra: Brahma-sūtra
Darshana: Darśana
Dharmakirti: Dharmakīrti
Dharma Shastra: Dharma-śāstra
Dignaga: Dignāga
Drishtanta: Dṛṣṭānta
Grahya-grahaka-vibhaga:
  Grāhya-grāhaka-vibhāga
Guna: Guṇa
Hetvabhasa: Hetvābhāsa
  (Hetu-ābhāsa)
Iccha: Icchā
Ishvara: Īśvara
Jati: Jāti
Jnana: Jñāna

Jnatata: Jñātatā
Kalpana: Kalpanā
Karaka: Kāraka
Kshanikatva: Kṣaṇikatva
Kumarila Bhatta: Kumārila
 Bhaṭṭa
Lakshana-artha: Lakṣaṇā-artha
Lakshanam: Lakṣaṇam
Lila: Līlā
Mandana Mishra: Maṇḍana
 Miśra
Maya: Māyā
Moksha: Mokṣa
Nagarjuna: Nāgārjuna
Nirakaravada: Nirākāravāda
Nirvana: Nirvāṇa
Nirvishesha: Nirviśeṣa
Nyaya: Nyāya
Padartha: Padārtha
Paksha: Pakṣa
Paratah Prakasha: Parataḥ
 Prakāśa
Paratah pramanya: Parataḥ
 prāmāṇya
Parinama
Paryudasa-pratishedha:
 Paryudāsa-pratiṣedha
Prabhakara Mishra: Prabhākara
 Miśra
Prakara: Prakāra
Prakashatman: Prakāśātman
Prama: Pramā
Pramana: Pramāṇa
Pramanya: Prāmāṇya
Pratyabhijna: Pratyabhijñā
Purusha: Puruṣa
Purushartha: Puruṣārtha
Purva Mimamsa: Pūrva
 Mīmāṃsā

Ramakantha Bhatta:
 Rāmakaṇṭha Bhaṭṭa
Ramanuja: Rāmānuja
Sadhya: Sādhya
Sakara-vada: Sākāra-vāda
Samanadhikaranya:
 Sāmānādhikaraṇya
Samanya: Sāmānya
Samanyato-drishta:
 Sāmānyato-dṛṣṭa
Samavaya: Samavāya
Samnyasa: Saṃnyāsa
Samsara: Saṃsāra
Sapaksha: Sapakṣa
Satkaryavada: Satkāryavāda
Sautrantika: Sautrāntika
Shaiva Siddhanta: Śaiva
 Siddhānta
Shakti: Śakti
Shankara: Śaṅkara (Śaṃkara)
Shantarakshita: Śāntarakṣita
Sheshavat: Śeṣavat
Shri Harsha: Śrī Harṣa
Shruti: Śrūti
Shunyata: Śūnyatā
Sphota: Sphoṭa
Svabhava: Svabhāva
Svalakshana: Svalakṣaṇa
Upadhi: Upādhi
Upanishad: Upaniṣad
Vaibhashika: Vaibhāṣika
Vaisheshika: Vaiśeṣika
Vedanta: Vedānta
Vijnanavada: Vijñānavāda
Vipaksha: Vipakṣa
Vishesha: Viśeṣa
Vishishta-advaita: Viśiṣṭa-advaita
Vyapti: Vyāpti
Yamuna

Bibliography

Anacker, S. (1984), *Seven Works of Vasubandhu*, Delhi: Motilal Banarsidass.

Balcerowicz, P. (2000), *Epistemology in Historical and Comparative Perspective*, Hamburg: Franz Steiner Verlag.

Bartley, C. J. (2002), *The Theology of Ramanuja*, London: Routledge-Curzon.

Bechert, H., and R. Gombrich (1984), *The World of Buddhism*, London: Thames and Hudson.

Betty, L. S. (1978), *Vadiraja's Refutation of Shankara's Non-Dualism*, Delhi: Motilal Banarsidass.

Bhattacharya, G. (1989), *Tarkasamgraha-dipika on Tarkasamgraha by Annambhatta*, Calcutta: Progressive Publishers.

Bhattacharya, K. (1998), *The Dialectical Method of Nagarjuna: Vigrahavyavartani*, Delhi: Motilal Banarsidass.

Bilimoria, P. (1988), *Sabdapramana: Word and Knowledge*, Dordrecht: Kluwer.

Brough, J. (1996a), 'Theories of General Linguistics in the Sanskrit Grammarians', in M. Hara and J. C. Wright (eds), *John Brough: Collected Papers*, London: SOAS, pp. 79–98.

Brough, J. (1996b), 'Some Indian Theories of Meaning', in M. Hara and J. C. Wright (eds), *John Brough: Collected Papers*, London: SOAS, pp. 114–29.

Buitenen, J. A. B. van (1953), *Ramanuja on the Bhagavad Gita*, The Hague: Smits.

Buitenen, J. A. B. van (1956), *Ramanuja's Vedarthasamgraha*, Poona: Deccan College.

Burton, D. (1999), *Emptiness Appraised: A Critical Study of Nagarjuna's Philosophy*, Richmond: Curzon.

Carman, J. B. (1974), *The Theology of Ramanuja*, New Haven: Yale University Press.

Chakrabarti, K. (1999), *Indian Philosophy of Mind: The Nyaya Dualist Tradition*, Albany: SUNY Press.

Chemparathy, G. (1972), *An Indian Rational Theology*, Vienna: De Nobili Research Library.

Clooney, F. X. (2001) *Hindu God, Christian God*, New York: Oxford University Press.

Collins, S. (1982), *Selfless Persons*, Cambridge: Cambridge University Press.

Conze, E. (1959), *Buddhist Scriptures*, Harmondsworth: Penguin.

Cowell, E. B., and A. E. Gough (1996), *The Sarva-darshana-samgraha of Madhavacharya or Review of the different systems of Hindu Philosophy*, Delhi: Motilal Banarsidass.

Crosby, K., and A. Skilton (trans.) (1996), *Shantideva: The Bodhicaryavatara*, Oxford: Oxford University Press.

Dumont, L. (1980), 'World Renunciation in Indian Religions', in L. Dumont, *Homo Hierarchicus*, Chicago: Chicago University Press.

Dundas, P. (1992), *The Jains*, London: Routledge.

Dunne, J. D. (2004), *Foundations of Dharmakirti's Philosophy*, Boston: Wisdom Publications.

Dyczkowski, M. (1987), *The Doctrine of Vibration: An Analysis of the Doctrines and Practices of Kashmir Shaivism*, Albany: SUNY Press.

Filliozat, P-S. (1994), *The Tantra of Svayambhu vidyapada with the commentary of Sadyojyoti*, Delhi: Motilal Banarsidass.

Flood, G. (1996), *Introduction to Hinduism*, Cambridge: Cambridge University Press.

Franco, E. (1994), *Perception, Knowledge and Disbelief*, Delhi: Motilal Banarsidass.

Frauwallner, E. (1995), *Studies in the Abhidharma Literature and the Origins of the Buddhist Philosophical Systems*, Albany: SUNY Press.

Ganeri, J. (1999), *Semantic Powers*, Oxford: Clarendon Press.

Ganeri, J. (2001a), *Philosophy in Classical India*, London: Routledge.

Ganeri, J. (2001b), *Indian Logic: A Reader*, London: Curzon.

Garfield, J. (1995), *The Fundamental Wisdom of the Middle Way*, New York: Oxford University Press.

Gerow, E. (1990), *The Jewel-Necklace of Argument*, New Haven: American Oriental Society.

Gerow, E. (2001), *The Vrttivarttika or Commentary on the Functions of Words of Appaya Dikshita*, New Haven: American Oriental Society.

Gethin, R. (1998), *Fundamentals of Buddhism*, Oxford: Oxford University Press.

Gombrich, R. (1996), *How Buddhism Began*, London: Athlone.

Gonda, J. (1975), *Vedic Literature*, Wiesbaden: Otto Harrassowitz.

Goodall, D. (1998), *Bhatta Ramakantha's Commentary on the Kiranatantra*, Pondichéry: École Française d'Extrême-Orient.

Goudriaan, T. (ed.) (1992), *Ritual and Speculation in Early Tantrism: Studies in Honour of André Padoux*, Albany: SUNY Press.

Granoff, P. (1978), *Philosophy and Argument in Late Vedanta: Shri Harsha's Khandanakhandakhadya*, Dordrecht: Reidel.

Halbfass, W. (1991), *Tradition and Reflection*, Albany: SUNY Press.

Halbfass, W. (1992, *On Being and What There Is: Classical Vaisheshika and the History of Indian Ontology*, Albany: SUNY Press.

Halbfass, W. (ed.) (1995), *Philology and Confrontation: Paul Hacker on Traditional and Modern Vedanta*, Albany: SUNY Press.

Hardy, F. (1983), *Viraha-Bhakti*, Delhi: Oxford University Press.

Hattori, M. (1968), *Dignaga, On Perception*, Cambridge, MA: Harvard University Press.

Hayes, R. (1988), *Dignaga on the Interpretation of Signs*, Dordrecht: Kluwer.

Hiriyanna, M. (1993), *Outline of Indian Philosophy*, Delhi: Motilal Banarsidass.

Hume, R. (1949), *The Thirteen Principal Upanishads*, Oxford: Oxford University Press.

Ingalls, D. H. H. (1951), *Materials for the Study of Navya-Nyaya Logic*, Cambridge, MA: Harvard University Press.

Ingalls, D. H. H., J. M. Masson and M. V. Patwardhan (trans.) (1990), *The Dhvanyaloka of Anandavardhana with the Locana of Abhinavagupta*, Cambridge, MA: Harvard University Press.

Jaini, P. S. (1979), *The Jaina Path of Purification*, Berkeley: University of California Press.

Jaini, P. S. (2000), *Collected Papers on Jaina Studies*, Delhi: Motilal Banarsidass.

Jha, G. (1911), *The Prabhakara School of Purva Mimamsa*, Allahabad: University of Allahabad Press.

Jha, G. (1964), *Purva Mimamsa in Its Sources*, Varanasi: Benares Hindu University Press.

Jha, G. (trans.) (1987), *The Tattvasamgraha of Shantarakshita with the Commentary of Kamalashila*, Vol. I, Baroda: Oriental Institute.

Jha, G. (trans.) (1988), *The Tattvasamgraha of Shantarakshita with the Commentary of Kamalashila*, Vol. II, Baroda: Oriental Institute.

Johnson, W. J. (1994), *The Bhagavad Gita*, Oxford: Oxford University Press.

Kahrs, E. (1998), *Indian Semantic Analysis*, Cambridge: Cambridge University Press.

Kajiyama, Y. (1998), *An Introduction to Buddhist Philosophy*, Wien: Universität Wien.

Karmarkar, R. D. (trans.) (1953), *Gaudapada-Karika*, Poona: Bhandarkar Oriental Research Institute.

Keown, D. (1992), *The Nature of Buddhist Ethics*, New York: St Martin's Press.

King, R. (1995), *Early Advaita Vedanta and Buddhism: The Mahayana Context of the Gaudapadiya-Karikas*, Albany: SUNY Press.

Larson, G. J. (1979), *Classical Samkhya*, Delhi: Motilal Banarsidass.

Larson, G. J., and R. S. Bhattacharya (eds) (1987), *Encyclopedia of Indian Philosophies: Samkhya*, Delhi: Motilal Banarsidass.

Lindtner, C. (1982), *Nagarjuniana*, Copenhagen: Akademisk Forlag.

Lipner, J. (1986), *The Face of Truth*, Basingstoke: Macmillan.

Lipner, J. (ed.) (1997), *The Fruits of Our Desiring*, Calgary: Bayeaux.

Matilal, B. K. (1968), *The Navya Nyaya Doctrine of Negation*, Cambridge, MA: Harvard University Press.

Matilal, B. K. (1981), *The Central Philosophy of Jainism*, Ahmedabad: L. D. Institute.

Matilal, B. K. (1986), *Perception: An Essay on Classical Indian Theories of Knowledge*, Oxford: Clarendon Press.

Matilal, B. K. (1990), *The Word and the World*, Delhi: Oxford University Press.

Matilal, B. K. (1998), *The Character of Logic in India*, Albany: SUNY Press.

Matilal, B. K. (2002a), *Ethics and Epics*, Delhi: Oxford University Press.

Matilal, B. K. (2002b), *Mind, Language and World*, Delhi: Oxford University Press.

Mayeda, S. (1979), *A Thousand Teachings*, Tokyo: Tokyo University Press.

Mesquita, R. (1988), *Yamunacarya's Samvitsiddhi*, Wien: Verlag der Osterreichischen Akademie der Wissenschaften.

Mesquita, R. (2000), *Madhva's Unknown Literary Sources: Some Observations*, Delhi: Aditya Prakashan.

Mohanty, J. N. (1966), *Gangesha's Theory of Truth*, Shantiniketan: Vishvabharati.

Mohanty, J. N. (1992), *Reason and Tradition in Indian Thought*, Oxford: Clarendon Press.

Mookerjee, S. (1975), *The Buddhist Philosophy of Universal Flux*, Delhi: Motilal Banarsidass.

Murti, T. R. V. (1955), *The Central Philosophy of Buddhism: A Study of the Madhyamika system*, London: George Allen and Unwin.

Neevel, W. G. (1977), *Yamuna's Vedanta and Pancaratra: Integrating the Classical and the Popular*, Montana: Scholar's Press.

O'Flaherty, W. (ed.) (1980), *Karma and Rebirth in Classical Indian Tradition*, Berkeley: University of California Press.

O'Flaherty, W. (1981), *The Rig Veda*, Harmondsworth: Penguin.

O'Flaherty, W. (1991), *The Laws of Manu*, Harmondsworth: Penguin.

Oetke, C. (1994), *Studies in the Doctrine of Trairupya*, Vienna: Universität Wien.

Olivelle, P. (1986), *Renunciation in Hinduism: A Medieval Debate*, Vienna: Universität Wien.

Olivelle, P. (1993), *The Ashrama System: The History and Hermeneutics of a Religious Institution*, New York: Oxford University Press.

Olivelle, P. (trans.) (1996), *Upanishads*, Oxford: Oxford University Press.

Olivelle, P. (trans.) (1999), *Dharmasutras: the Law Codes of Apastamba, Gautama, Baudhayana and Vasistha, Translated from the Original Sanskrit*, Oxford: Oxford University Press.

Padoux, A. (1990), *Vac: The Concept of the Word in Selected Hindu Tantras*, Albany: SUNY Press.

Pandey, K. C. (trans.) (1986), *Ishvara-pratyabhijna-vimarshini of Abhinavagupta: Doctrine of Divine Recognition*, Delhi: Motilal Banarsidass.

Phillips, S. H. (1996), *Classical Indian Metaphysics*, La Salle: Open Court.

Potter, K. H. (trans.) (1957), *The Padarthatattvanirupanam of Raghunatha Shiromani (A Demonstration of the True Nature of the Things to Which Words Refer)*, Cambridge, MA: Harvard University Press.

Potter, K. H. (ed.)(1977), *Encyclopedia of Indian Philosophies: Vol. II, Indian Metaphysics and Epistemology: The Tradition of Nyaya-Vaisheshika up to Gangesha*, Delhi: Motilal Banarsidass.

Potter, K. H. (ed.) (1981), *Encyclopedia of Indian Philosophies: Vol. III, Advaita Vedanta up to Shankara and His Pupils*, Delhi: Motilal Banarsidass.

Potter, K. H. (1996), *Encyclopedia of Indian Philosophies: Vol. VII, Abhidharma Buddhism to 150 CE*, Delhi: Motilal Banarsidass.

Potter, K. H., and S. Bhattacharya (eds) (1993), *Encyclopedia of Indian Philosophies: Vol. VI, Indian Philosophical Analysis; Nyaya Vaisheshika from Gangesha to Raghunatha Shiromani*, Delhi: Motilal Banarsidass.

Prasad, Rajendra (2002), *Dharmakirti's Theory of Inference: Revaluation and Reconstruction*, Delhi: Oxford University Press.

Pruden, L. (1988), *Abhidharmakoshabhashyam*, Berkeley: Asian Humanities Press.

Radhakrishnan, S. (1953), *The Principal Upanishads*, London: George Allen and Unwin.

Radhakrishnan, S., and C. A. Moore (eds) (1957), *A Sourcebook in Indian Philosophy*, Princeton: Princeton University Press.

Rahula, W. (1969), *What the Buddha Taught*, London: Gordon Fraser.

Ram-Prasad, C. (2001), *Knowledge and Liberation in Classical Indian Thought*, Basingstoke: Palgrave Macmillan.

Ram-Prasad, C. (2002), *Advaita Epistemology and Metaphysics*, London: RoutledgeCurzon.

Rocher, L. (ed.) (1988), *Studies in Indian Literature and Philosophy: Collected Articles of J. A. B. van Buitenen*, Delhi: Motilal Banarsidass.

Ruegg D. S. (1981), *The Literature of the Madhyamaka School of Philosophy in India*, Wiesbaden: Otto Harrassowitz.

Sanderson, Alexis (1985), 'Purity and Power among the Brahmins of Kashmir', in M. Carrithers, S. Collins and S. Lukes (eds), *The Category of the Person*, Cambridge: Cambridge University Press, pp. 190–216.

Sanderson, Alexis (1990), 'Shaivism and the Tantric Traditions', in F. Hardy (ed.), *The World's Religions: The Religions of Asia*, London: Routledge, pp. 128–72.

Sanderson, Alexis (1992), 'The Doctrine of the Malinivijayottaratantra', in T. Goudriaan (ed.), *Ritual and Speculation in Early Tantrism: Studies in Honor of André Padoux*, Albany: SUNY Press, pp. 281–312.

Sarma, D. (2003), *An Introduction to Madhva Vedanta*, Aldershot: Ashgate.

Sharma, B. N. K. (1986), *Philosophy of Shri Madhvacharya*, Delhi: Motilal Banarsidass.

Shastri, G. (1959), *The Philosophy of Word and Meaning*, Calcutta: Sanskrit College.

Siderits, M. (1991), *Indian Philosophy of Language: Selected Issues*, Dordrecht: Kluwer.

Siderits, M. (2003), *Personal Identity and Buddhist Philosophy: Empty Persons*, Aldershot: Ashgate.

Singh, J. (1980), *Spanda Karikas*, Delhi: Motilal Banarsidass.

Singh, J. (1982), *Pratyabhijnahridayam*, Delhi: Motilal Banarsidass.

Stcherbatsky, Th. [1930] (1993), *Buddhist Logic*, Vol. II, Delhi: Motilal Banarsidass.

Stcherbatsky, Th. [1936] (1970), *Madhyanta-Vibhanga*, Osnabruck: Biblio Verlag.

Suryanarayana Shastri, S. S. (trans.) (1942), *Vedantaparibhasha*, Adyar: The Adyar Library and Research Centre.

Tachikawa, M. (1981), *The Structure of the World in Udayana's Realism*, Dordrecht: Reidel.

Thibaut, G. (trans.) (1904a), *The Vedanta-Sutras with the Commentary of Ramanuja*, Oxford: Clarendon Press.

Thibaut, G. (trans.) (1904b), *The Vedanta-Sutras with the Commentary of Shankaracarya*, 2 vols, Oxford: Clarendon Press.

Thrasher, A. W. (1993), *The Advaita Vedanta of Brahma-siddhi*, Delhi: Motilal Banarsidass.

Tillemans, T. J. F. (1999), *Scripture, Logic and Language*, Boston: Wisdom Publications.

Torella, R. (2002), *The Ishvarapratyabhijnakarika of Utpaladeva*, Delhi: Motilal Banarsidass.

Vattanky, J. (1984), *Gangesha's Philosophy of God*, Madras: Adyar Library.

Whicher, I. (1998), *The Integrity of the Yoga Darshana: A Reconsideration of Classical Yoga*, Albany: SUNY Press.

White, D. G. (2003), *The Kiss of the Yogini*, Chicago: University of Chicago Press.

Williams, P. (1989), *Mahayana Buddhism*, London: Routledge.

Williams, P. (1998), *Altruism and Reality*, London: Curzon Press.

Wood, T. E. (1991), *Mind Only: A Philosophical and Doctrinal Analysis of the Vijnanavada*, Honolulu: University of Hawaii Press.

Woods, J. H. (1927), *The Yoga Sutras*, Cambridge, MA: Harvard University Press.

Zaehner, R. C. (1969), *The Bhagavad Gita*, Oxford: Oxford University Press.